SELECTED

JOHN DONNE

THE POETRY BOOKSHELF

General Editor: James Reeves

Martin Seymour-Smith: *Shakespeare's Sonnets*
James Reeves: *John Donne*
Jack Dalglish: *Eight Metaphysical Poets*
James Reeves and Martin Seymour-Smith: *Andrew Marvell*
Roger Sharrock: *John Dryden*
F. W. Bateson: *William Blake*
Roger Sharrock: *William Wordsworth*
James Reeves: *S. T. Coleridge*
Robin Skelton: *Lord Byron*
John Holloway: *P. B. Shelley*
Robert Gittings: *Poems and Letters of John Keats*
Edmund Blunden: *Alfred Lord Tennyson*
James Reeves: *Emily Dickinson*
James Reeves: *G. M. Hopkins*
James Reeves: *The Modern Poets' World*
James Reeves: *D. H. Lawrence*
John Heath Stubbs: *Selected Poems of Alexander Pope*

SELECTED POEMS OF
JOHN
DONNE

Edited with an Introduction
Notes and Commentary

by

JAMES REEVES

HEINEMANN

Heinemann Educational Books Ltd
Halley Court, Jordan Hill, Oxford OX2 8EJ
OXFORD LONDON EDINBURGH
MELBOURNE SYDNEY AUCKLAND
IBADAN NAIROBI GABORONE HARARE
KINGSTON PORTSMOUTH NH(USA)
SINGAPORE MADRID

JOHN DONNE 1571-1631

ISBN 0 435 15003 0

FIRST PUBLISHED 1952
REPRINTED IN LARGER FORMAT 1958
REPRINTED 1961, 1963, 1966, 1967, 1969,
1970, 1972
REPRINTED WITH CORRECTIONS 1974
REPRINTED 1977, 1978, 1981, 1985, 1986, 1987, 1989, 1991

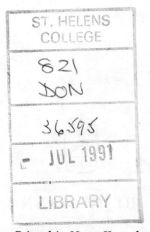
Printed in Hong Kong by
Dah Hua Printing Press Co., Ltd.

CONTENTS

INTRODUCTION

THE plan of this selection from the poems of Donne needs
some explanation. It consists of those poems which are
most likely to appeal to general readers, as distinct from
scholars and specialists. I have included the bulk of the
Songs and Sonets; several of the so-called *Elegies*, some
of them popular but most of them much less widely
known; several miscellaneous pieces; and a selection
from the religious verse. I have omitted the *Satires* and
the philosophical poems, because these seem to me, as
well as to most other readers, poetically far inferior;
their appeal is to curiosity rather than to the poetic
sense, and their place is not in an introductory selection
like the present. Little is here included which should
distract attention from Donne at his greatest, his most
poetic.

The other special feature of this edition is the Notes
and Commentary, which are fuller than in any other
edition I know of. Much has been written in a general
way about Donne and his poetry, but it seems to me
important to focus attention on the poems themselves.
They are difficult to understand, but they are worth
considerable effort of interpretation, especially on the
intellectual side. I know from experience in teaching
that many readers retain a sharp and vivid impression
of the beauty of Donne's poems without an equally clear
idea of their meaning as a whole; they remember single
lines or short passages. Between the most striking and
most immediately comprehensible lines there are often
passages of great intellectual complexity which require
some pains to understand; without such understanding,
the poems cannot be fully appreciated. Rather than
attempt to explain isolated phrases, lines and allusions

I have in many cases found it more satisfactory to attempt a sort of summary paraphrase of the poem as a whole, dealing more fully with the complex, than with the straightforward passages. This may seem to some readers tedious, but it is hoped that they will put up with it for the sake of others who find the intellectual thread of the poems elusive and tangled. I ought to add that there are places where I find the meaning almost, if not quite, escapes elucidation, and no other edition has proved helpful. It is here that I must acknowledge my indebtedness to Sir Herbert Grierson, to whose great work in establishing, and at many points elucidating, the text of the poems all readers of Donne owe so much. His two volume Oxford edition of 1912 remains the standard text to which all who wish to make a special study must turn.

John Donne (pronounced *Dunne*) lived at a time when life for men of his class might be adventurous, even dangerous, and in many ways uncertain. It was an age of rapid social change, when fortunes were made and lost quickly; when the most dazzling success might be followed by sudden and complete disgrace. It was an age of acute religious controversy and uncertainty, an age of war and foreign danger, an age when the monarchy—the apex of social and political organisation— was in constant danger; it was an age of spies and informers, intriguers, adventurers, careerists. It was, moreover, an age of rapid and prodigious artistic growth. The theatre of Marlowe, Shakespeare, Webster and Jonson rose, flourished, and fell into decline within the span of two generations. Donne was born in 1571, a few years before the building of the first permanent playhouse in London. He was a Londoner, the son of Roman Catholic parents. At thirteen he went to Oxford and at sixteen to Cambridge. From twenty to twenty-five he lived in London as an "Inns of Court man", ostensibly studying law first at Thavies Inn and then at Lincolns

Inn. It is the "Jack Donne" of this period of whom we would like to know more, for this was probably the period of many, if not most, of the *Songs and Sonets*.

Contemporary records of Donne at this period are scanty. We can do best by supplementing the knowledge to be inferred from the poems by what we know of the life of an "Inns of Court man" of the time. Ben Jonson tells us that most of Donne's best pieces were written by the time he was twenty-five—that is, by 1596. This can hardly be true; nevertheless, it is probable that by this date many of his satires were circulating in manuscript—very few of his poems were printed during his lifetime—and he had earned a reputation as a brilliant, cynical wit with a vein of realistic love poetry quite unlike anything else that was then in fashion.

It was about 1595 that Shakespeare wrote his first great romantic tragedy, *Romeo and Juliet*. I have mentioned the drama in connection with Donne's life, because the adventurous figures of the time are likely to be those reflected in the plays. For all its Veronese setting *Romeo and Juliet* is a play of contemporary London, where feuds between the great houses might well break out in the street brawling with which this tragedy opens. If we look at the group of young men in the rival houses of Montague and Capulet, we shall find a portrait of the typical young gallants of Donne's London. Donne might well have been the companion of Romeo, Benvolio, Mercutio or Tybalt. As a wit he would have given Mercutio a run for his money; as a lover he might have rivalled Romeo, and would certainly have railed at him for his idealistic infatuation with Rosaline as unmercifully and as bawdily as Mercutio and Benvolio. He might have been as ready with his sword as Tybalt; what we would now consider less manly, he could certainly have given way to a tearful hysteria as undignified as Romeo's before Friar Laurence. The prevalence of tears in Donne's poetry and in Elizabethan

drama generally is an indication as striking as any of the
temperamental difference between that age and this. It
is now the British tradition for men to be stoical and not
weep. The control and suppression of emotion are now
taken for granted. In such a tradition neither Shakes-
peare's plays nor Donne's poems could have been as
they are. True, a Shakespearian character, overcome
by the loss of a wife, a child or a friend, apologised for his
"unmanly drops", but the frequency with which these
drops are mentioned indicates a temperamental habit by
which emotions were very near the surface, and might
readily erupt as violence, hysteria or poetry. "The
spontaneous overflow of powerful feelings" is a phrase
which applies more nearly to Donne's poetry than to
that of any other writer.

In one respect, the young men of the Montagues and
Capulets would have been out of their depth with their
contemporary. Donne was passionately intellectual,
and he must have been so at all times. It is a charac-
teristic of his poems which all critics have noted, and
which indeed forms one of his chief claims to uniqueness,
that feeling and intellect are never for long separated:
or rather, that if one of them is exhibited by itself in
any of his poems, it is always intellect, never emotion.
Where his poetry becomes tedious is where feeling is
absent and the writing is merely clever. There is no
doubt that cleverness for its own sake was admired by
Donne's contemporaries. But in Donne's poems at
their best, intellect never gets out of hand; there is,
throughout, "the spontaneous overflow of powerful
feelings". Intellect and emotion are inseparably united,
they exist in harmony, not in opposition. In the poems
of Wordsworth, for instance, or Shelley, or other
romantic poets, there is tension between the two, rarely
union. Donne could never have sighed, as Keats did
"O for a life of sensations rather than of thoughts!" To
him thought at its best *was* sensation. The unthinking

lyricism of, say, Burns' "My love is like a red, red rose" no longer fully satisfies the adult reader, because he knows and thinks too much. There is an innocence, a simplicity about all purely emotional love-lyrics that makes them belong to a range of experience which is not that of the modern intellectual reader, because it is both unattainable and at the same time limited. In appreciating the *Songs and Sonets*, a modern reader need not forget that he has a brain; and he is constantly reminded that he has emotions. An excess of intellect makes love poems impossible, its absence makes them inadequate. Except perhaps for Shakespeare in some of his sonnets, Donne is the only writer of love poems who achieves this miraculous balance.

What the young Donne achieved in love poems was very nearly impossible. It was achieved against the poetical fashion of his day and almost against love itself. It was the fashion to write love poems in the artificial style of Petrarch, idealising the lady and falsifying the poet. The lady was placed on a pedestal of unapproachable perfection, at the foot of which the lover sighed, swooned, and in extreme cases died. Donne not only knew that love is not like this; he had the originality to write poems in a new and realistic vein. So realistic was he about the nature of women and of the various passions and appetites designated in the word "love", that much of his poetry was harsh, cynical and bitter.

> I am two fooles, I know,
> For loving, and for saying so
>   In whining Poëtry;

> I can love her, and her, and you and you,
> I can love any, so she be not true.

> Hope not for minde in women; at their best
> Sweetnesse and wit, they, are but *Mummy*, possest.

Some of what Donne wrote in this vein was written deliberately to shock, and to please by shocking; yet it is difficult to be certain that anything he wrote was insincere and not strongly felt at least at the moment of writing. There never was more spontaneous poetry—poetry that gives the impression of being written while the emotion was still overpowering. Some of it was undeniably written as an escape from emotion. What the *Songs and Sonets* give us is a day-to-day picture of a restless and demonstrative temperament, experiencing all the moods of a passionate lover, from a lofty intellectual rapture, through delighted physical satisfaction, down to a sated and almost morbid disgust. This last mood is at times felt so strongly and expressed so violently, so brutally, that the wonder is how the same mind can have experienced emotion at the opposite pole.

> Let not thy divining heart
>   Forethinke me any ill,
> Destiny may take thy part
>   And may thy feares fulfill;
>   But thinke that wee
> Are but turned aside to sleepe;
> They who one another keepe
>   Alive, ne'r parted bee.
>
> All other things, to their destruction draw,
>   Only our love hath no decay;
> This, no to morrow hath, nor yesterday,
> Running it never runs from us away,
> But truly keepes his first, last, everlasting day
>
> If, as I have, you also doe
>   Vertue 'attir'd in woman see,
> And dare love that, and say so too.
>   And forget the Hee and Shee; . . .

Much speculation has been exercised, and very little

information discovered, about Donne's relations with women at this time. In his later years he speaks in tones of shocked confession of his "profane mistresses", and his first biographer, Walton, was more than reticent. Yet it is possible that Donne exaggerated here, as in everything else. His was a nature which could scarcely express itself except through hyperbole. This came as naturally to him as under-statement to a Chinese poet. It may be inferred that whether his affairs were few and protracted, or—as seems more likely—many and short lived, it is obvious that he knew women of various characters, from the shallowest to the most sensitive. It is known that he later formed close and admiring friendships with noble ladies of the highest reputation, such as Lady Magdalen Herbert and the Countess of Bedford. But the central and determining relation of his life was that with his wife, Anne More.

When Donne was about twenty-two, his brother Henry was arrested for pro-Catholic activities and died in Newgate prison. This event must have reminded Donne tragically of the danger of his position as one with Catholic associations. On the death of his father about this time he inherited his own, and soon afterwards his brother's, portion of the estate; this gave him independence for a time, and he was enabled to travel on the continent. He was thus put in direct touch with the new ideas and fashions for which his eager intellectual curiosity sought, and which find continual expression in his poems. In 1596 and 1597 he went, like other men of adventurous mind, with Essex on his expedition to Cadiz and later to the Azores.

From 1598 to 1602 he had his first regular salaried employment as secretary in the household of Sir Thomas Egerton, an important government official. For any ordinary Elizabethan careerist, provided he did not let his Catholic associations interfere, this would have presented the prospect of a possibly dazzling future either in politics, or, if his turn of mind had led him in that direction, in the church. But Donne effectually compromised any immediate possibility of advancement by an imprudent and secret marriage with his employer's niece, Anne More. The marriage took place in 1601, and when it was discovered the following year, Donne was dismissed and his wife's outraged father had him imprisoned in the Fleet. Reconciliation and release took place before long, but it was followed by a period of poverty with his wife and dependence on the patronage of the great. For many years Donne's chief intellectual energy was occupied in writing religious controversy. At length, after prolonged pressure from his ecclesiastical patrons, he became reconciled with the Anglican church, and in 1615 he took holy orders. Did Donne accept Anglican doctrine for the sake of material security? This is a question which no one can now answer, and which probably no one, certainly not Donne himself, could ever have answered. In any case it has little to do with us here. For the rest of his life Donne was a devoted and sincere churchman; on the intellectual side his conversion was complete and unswerving. If he felt at times the emotional pull of his Catholic childhood, this is scarcely to be wondered at in a nature so incessantly introspective and so impatient of compromise and half-truth.

We shall never know for certain which of his love poems are addressed to his wife, but from the tone of those few about which we can be more or less certain, it is clear that his love for her was tender and whole-hearted. With her he found that balance between platonic admiration and physical fulfilment which he had been seeking in vain and without rest in his earlier relationships. When in 1617 she died in childbirth, the sole remaining passion of his life was his devotion to the church. He gradually obtained that position of eminence to which his mind and zeal entitled him, and after successive smaller appointments he was made Dean of St. Paul's at the age of fifty. During the remaining ten years of his life almost everything he wrote and said was marked by gloom, austerity and a stoical acceptance of the divine will. At the time of his death in 1631 he was the most famous preacher of his day.

Just as in his early manhood Donne personified much of the temper of his age—adventurous, impulsive, passionate in thought and action, witty, daring, extravagant—so too in his later austerity he was a man of his time. The intellectual Englishman of the reign of James I was, in comparison, sombre, melancholy. sermon-loving. Donne, like other thoughtful men of his time, was "much possessed by death".

In this brief sketch of the life and poetry of Donne there are many omissions which it is hoped the interested reader will supply for himself from fuller sources. Little has been said about his learning: this was perhaps broader than it was deep, and less of it is drawn on in the poems than is commonly thought. The allusions to theology, astrology, medicine, the law, natural history and classical myth are frequent; but they are introduced not for their intrinsic fascination but for their aptness to the immediate purpose of a poem. Donne was interested in all knowledge, old and new, but he was no antiquarian and no amateur of novelty for fashion's sake.

Something must be said about Donne's versification, since this has aroused the notice of critics of all times, from those of Donne himself to the present day. Nearly all critics, from Jonson and Dryden to the romantics and Victorians have felt it necessary to comment on, and in some cases excuse, what they have called the "harshness" of Donne's verse. This is because the ideal has at all times been a Spenserian smoothness. This Donne deliberatedly avoided; either he could not write smoothly or he did not care to. The metrical roughness of some of his lines, the violent departures from the rhythmic pattern, the angularity of his style are a deliberate reflection of his erratic and nervous temperament. Of no writer is it truer to say that "the style is the man". Our own age values him more highly on this account. We like his roughness and we would not wish it otherwise. We feel that it is the man himself speaking, if not to us, to those nameless and enigmatic beings whose ghosts appear so startlingly in his tortured lines. Donne's rhythms, his vocabulary—at times so odd, at times so simple, the twists and perplexities of his syntax, his metaphors and paradoxes, his unpredictable vagaries of thought and feeling—these *are* Donne's poetry. To wish that he had written differently is to wish that he had been a different man, or that he had not fully realised himself, as we are bound to believe he did. It has been pointed out that he prepared none of his poems for the press and that if he had done so he would have smoothed out some of the irregularities.

This last is a very doubtful assumption. Equally doubtful is the assumption that his poems would thus have been improved.

The history of Donne's reputation during the past three and a half centuries is an interesting one, which it is impossible to touch on here.[1] Nor is it possible to go into the reasons why the present age has made Donne peculiarly its own. It is enough to say that for the first time since his own day critics are able to praise and value Donne for those very qualities which the intervening generations have regarded as blemishes.

[1] It may be studied briefly in the admirable selections from critics given at the beginning of Professor Garrod's *John Donne: Poetry and Prose*. (Clarendon Press).

SELECTED POEMS

THE GOOD-MORROW

I wonder by my troth, what thou, and I
Did, till we lov'd? were we not wean'd till then?
But suck'd on countrey pleasures, childishly?
Or snorted we in the seaven sleepers den?
T'was so; But this, all pleasures fancies bee.
If ever any beauty I did see,
Which I desir'd, and got, t'was but a dreame of thee.

And now good morrow to our waking soules,
Which watch not one another out of feare;
For love, all love of other sights controules,
And makes one little roome, an every where.
Let sea-discoverers to new worlds have gone,
Let Maps to other, worlds on worlds have showne,
Let us possesse one world, each hath one, and is one.

My face in thine eye, thine in mine appeares,
And true plaine hearts doe in the faces rest,
Where can we finde two better hemispheares
Without sharpe North, without declining West?
What ever dyes, was not mixt equally;
If our two loves be one, or, thou and I
Love so alike, that none doe slacken, none can die.

SONG

Goe, and catche a falling starre,
    Get with child a mandrake roote,
Tell me, where all past yeares are,
    Or who cleft the Divels foot,

Teach me to heare Mermaides singing,
  Or to keep off envies stinging,
        And finde
        What winde
Serves to advance an honest minde.

If thou beest borne to strange sights,
  Things invisible to see,
Ride ten thousand daies and nights,
  Till age snow white haires on thee,
Thou, when thou retorn'st, wilt tell mee
All strange wonders that befell thee,
        And sweare
        No where
Lives a woman true, and faire.

If thou findst one, let mee know,
  Such a Pilgrimage were sweet;
Yet doe not, I would not goe,
  Though at next doore wee might meet,
Though shee were true, when you met her,
And last, till you write your letter,
        Yet shee
        Will bee
False, ere I come, to two, or three.

THE UNDERTAKING

I HAVE done one braver thing
  Than all the *Worthies* did,
And yet a braver thence doth spring,
  Which is, to keepe that hid.

It were but madnes now t'impart
  The skill of specular stone,
When he which can have learn'd the art
  To cut it, can finde none.

So, if I now should utter this,
    Others (because no more
Such stuffe to worke upon, there is,)
    Would love but as before.

But he who lovelinesse within
    Hath found, all outward loathes,
For he who colour loves, and skinne,
    Loves but their oldest clothes.

If, as I have, you also doe
    Vertue'attir'd in woman see,
And dare love that, and say so too,
    And forget the Hee and Shee;

And if this love, though placed so,
    From prophane men you hide,
Which will no faith on this bestow,
    Or, if they doe, deride:

Then you have done a braver thing
    Than all the *Worthies* did;
And a braver thence will spring,
    Which is, to keepe that hid.

THE SUNNE RISING

Busie old foole, unruly Sunne,
    Why dost thou thus,
Through windowes, and through curtaines call on us?
Must to thy motions lovers seasons run?
    Sawcy pedantique wretch, goe chide
    Late schoole boyes, and sowre prentices,
  Goe tell Court-huntsmen, that the King will ride,
  Call countrey ants to harvest offices;
Love, all alike, no season knowes, nor clyme,
Nor houres, dayes, moneths, which are the rags of time.

Thy beames, so reverend, and strong
  Why shouldst thou thinke?
I could eclipse and cloud them with a winke.
But that I would not lose her sight so long:
  If her eyes have not blinded thine,
    Looke, and to morrow late, tell mee,
  Whether both the'India's of spice and Myne
  Be where thou leftst them, or lie here with mee
Aske for those Kings whom thou saw'st yesterday,
And thou shalt heare, All here in one bed lay.

    She'is all States, and all Princes, I,
      Nothing else is.
Princes doe but play us; compar'd to this,
All honor's mimique; All wealth alchimie.
      Thou sunne art halfe as happy'as wee,
        In that the world's contracted thus;
      Thine age askes ease, and since thy duties bee
      To warme the world, that's done in warming us.
Shine here to us, and thou art every where;
This bed thy centre is, these walls, thy spheare.

THE INDIFFERENT

I CAN love both faire and browne,
Her whom abundance melts, and her whom want betraies
Her who loves lonenesse best, and her who maskes and
    plaies,
Her whom the country form'd, and whom the town,
Her who beleeves, and her who tries,
Her who still weepes with spungie eyes,
And her who is dry corke, and never cries;
I can love her, and her, and you and you,
I can love any, so she be not true.

Will no other vice content you?
Wil it not serve your turn to do, as did your mothers?
Or have you all old vices spent, and now would finde out
    others?
Or doth a feare, that men are true, torment you?
Oh we are not, be not you so,
Let mee, and doe you, twenty know.
Rob mee, but binde me not, and let me goe
Must I, who came to travaile thorow you,
Grow your fixt subject, because you are true?

Venus heard me sigh this song,
And by Loves sweetest Part, Variety, she swore,
She heard not this till now; and that it should be so no
    more.
She went, examin'd, and return'd ere long,
And said, alas, Some two or three
Poore Heretiques in love there bee,
Which thinke to stablish dangerous constancie.
But I have told them, since you will be true,
You shall be true to them, who'are false to you.

LOVES USURY

For every houre that thou wilt spare mee now,
    I will allow.
Usurious God of Love, twenty to thee,
When with my browne, my gray haires equall bee;
Till then, Love, let my body raigne, and let
Mee travell, sojourne, snatch, plot, have, forget,
Resume my last yeares relict: thinke that yet
      We'had never met.

Let mee thinke any rivalls letter mine,
    And at next nine

Keepe midnights promise; mistake by the way
The maid, and tell the Lady of that delay;
Onely let mee love none, no, not the sport;
From country grasse, to comfitures of Court,
Or cities quelque choses, let report
          My minde transport.

This bargaine's good; if when I'am old, I bee
          Inflam'd by thee,
If thine owne honour, or my shame, or paine,
Thou covet, most at that age thou shalt gaine.
Doe thy will then, then subject and degree,
And fruit of love, Love I submit to thee,
Spare mee till then, I'll beare it, though she bee
          One that loves mee.

THE CANONIZATION

For Godsake hold your tongue, and let me love,
          Or chide my palsie, or my gout,
My five gray haires, or ruin'd fortune flout,
     With wealth your state, your minde with Arts
          improve,
          Take you a course, get you a place,
          Observe his honour, or his grace,
Or the Kings reall, or his stamped face
     Contemplate, what you will, approve,
     So you will let me love.

Alas, alas, who's injur'd by my love?
     What merchants ships have my sighs drown'd?
Who saies my teares have overflow'd his ground?
     When did my colds a forward spring remove?
          When did the heats which my veines fill
          Adde one more to the plaguie Bill?
Soldiers finde warres, and Lawyers finde out still

Litigious men, which quarrels move,
Though she and I do love.

Call us what you will, wee are made such by love;
    Call her one, mee another flye,
We'are Tapers too, and at our owne cost die,
    And wee in us finde the'Eagle and the Dove.
        The Phœnix ridle hath more wit
        By us, we two being one, are it.
So to one neutrall thing both sexes fit,
    Wee dye and rise the same, and prove
    Mysterious by this love.

Wee can dye by it, if not live by love,
    And if unfit for tombes and hearse
Our legend bee, it will be fit for verse;
    And if no peece of Chronicle wee prove,
        We'll build in sonnets pretty roomes;
        As well a well wrought urne becomes
The greatest ashes, as halfe-acre tombes,
    And by these hymnes, all shall approve
    Us *Canoniz'd* for Love:

And thus invoke us; You whom reverend love
    Made one anothers hermitage:
You, to whom love was peace, that now is rage;
    Who did the whole worlds soule contract, and drove
        Into the glasses of your eyes
        (So made such mirrors, and such spies,
That they did all to you epitomize,)
    Countries, Townes, Courts: Beg from above
    A patterne of your love!

THE TRIPLE FOOLE

I AM two fooles, I know,
For loving, and for saying so
   In whining Poëtry;
But where's that wiseman, that would not be I,
   If she would not deny?
Then as th'earths inward narrow crooked lanes
Do purge sea waters fretfull salt away,
   I thought, if I could draw my paines,
Through Rimes vexation, I should them allay.
Griefe brought to numbers cannot be so fierce,
For, he tames it, that fetters it in verse.

   But when I have done so,
Some man, his art and voice to show,
   Doth Set and sing my paine,
And, by delighting many, frees againe
   Griefe, which verse did restraine.
To Love, and Griefe tribute of Verse belongs
But not of such as pleases when'tis read,
   Both are increased by such songs:
For both their triumphs so are published,
And I, which was two fooles, do so grow three:
Who are a little wise, the best fooles bee.

LOVERS INFINITENESSE

IF yet I have not all thy love,
Deare, I shall never have it all,
I cannot breath one other sigh, to move,
Nor can intreat one other teare to fall,
And all my treasure, which should purchase thee,

Sighs, teares, and oathes, and letters I have spent.
Yet no more can be due to mee,
Than at the bargaine made was ment,
If then thy gift of love were partiall,
That some to mee, some should to others fall,
   Deare, I shall never have Thee All.

Or if then thou gavest mee all,
All was but All, which thou hadst then;
But if in thy heart, since, there be or shall,
New love created bee, by other men,
Which have their stocks intire, and can in teares,
In sighs, in oathes, and letters outbid mee,
This new love may beget new feares,
For, this love was not vowed by thee.
And yet it was, thy gift being generall,
The ground, thy heart is mine, what ever shall
   Grow there, deare, I should have it all.

Yet I would not have all yet,
Hee that hath all can have no more,
And since my love doth every day admit
New growth, thou shouldst have new rewards in
   store;
Thou canst not every day give me thy heart,
If thou canst give it, then thou never gavest it:
Loves riddles are, that though thy heart depart,
It stayes at home, and thou with losing savest it:
But wee will have a way more liberall,
Than changing hearts, to joyne them, so wee shall
   Be one, and one anothers All.

SONG

SWEETEST love, I do not goe
　　For wearinesse of thee,
Nor in hope the world can show
　　A fitter Love for mee;
　　　　But since that I
Must dye at last, 'tis best,
To use my selfe in jest
　　　Thus by fain'd deaths to dye;

Yesternight the Sunne went hence,
　　And yet is here to day,
He hath no desire nor sense,
　　Nor halfe so short a way:
　　　　Then feare not mee,
But beleeve that I shall make
Speedier journeyes, since I take
　　　More wings and spurres than hee.

O how feeble is mans power,
　　That if good fortune fall,
Cannot adde another houre,
　　Nor a lost houre recall!
　　　　But come bad chance,
And wee joyne to'it our strength,
And wee teach it art and length,
　　　It selfe o'r us to'advance.

When thou sigh'st, thou sigh'st not winde,
　　But sigh'st my soule away,
When thou weep'st, unkindly kinde,
　　My lifes blood doth decay.
　　　　It cannot bee
That thou lov'st mee, as thou say'st,
If in thine my life thou waste,
　　　That art the best of mee.

Let not thy divining heart
  Forethinke me any ill,
Destiny may take thy part,
  And may thy feares fulfill;
    But thinke that wee
Are but turn'd aside to sleepe;
They who one another keepe
  Alive, ne'r parted bee

A FEAVER

OH doe not die, for I shall hate
  All women so, when thou art gone,
That thee I shall not celebrate,
  When I remember, thou wast one.

But yet thou canst not die, I know,
  To leave this world behinde, is death,
But when thou from this world wilt goe,
  The whole world vapors with thy breath.

Or if, when thou, the worlds soule, goest,
  It stay, tis but thy carkasse then,
The fairest woman, but thy ghost,
  But corrupt wormes, the worthyest men.

O wrangling schooles, that search what fire
  Shall burne this world, had none the wit
Unto this knowledge to aspire,
  That this her feaver might be it?

And yet she cannot wast by this,
  Nor long beare this torturing wrong,
For much corruption needfull is
  To fuell such a feaver long.

These burning fits but meteors bee,
   Whose matter in thee is soone spent.
Thy beauty,'and all parts, which are thee,
   Are unchangeable firmament.

Yet t'was of my minde, seising thee,
   Though it in thee cannot persever.
For I had rather owner bee
   Of thee one houre, than all else ever.

AIRE AND ANGELS

Twice or thrice had I loved thee,
Before I knew thy face or name;
So in a voice, so in a shapelesse flame,
Angells affect us oft, and worship'd bee;
   Still when, to where thou wert, I came,
Some lovely glorious nothing I did see.
   But since my soule, whose child love is,
Takes limmes of flesh, and else could nothing doe,
   More subtile than the parent is,
Love must not be, but take a body too,
   And therefore what thou wert, and who,
     I bid Love aske, and now
That it assume thy body, I allow,
And fixe it selfe in thy lip, eye, and brow.

Whilst thus to ballast love, I thought,
And so more steddily to have gone,
With wares which would sinke admiration,
I saw, I had loves pinnace overfraught,
   Ev'ry thy haire for love to worke upon
Is much too much, some fitter must be sought;
     For, nor in nothing, nor in things
Extreme, and scatt'ring bright, can love inhere;

Then as an Angell, face, and wings
Of aire, not pure as it, yet pure doth weare,
  So thy love may be my loves spheare;
    Just such disparitie
As is twixt Aire and Angells puritie,
'Twixt womens love, and mens will ever bee.

BREAKE OF DAY

'Tis true, 'tis day; what though it be?
O wilt thou therefore rise from me?
Why should we rise, because 'tis light?
Did we lie downe, because 'twas night?
Love which in spight of darknesse brought us
  hether,
Should in despight of light keepe us together.

Light hath no tongue, but is all eye;
If it could speake as well as spie,
This were the worst, that it could say,
That being well, I faine would stay,
And that I lov'd my heart and honor so,
That I would not from him, that had them, goe.

Must businesse thee from hence remove?
Oh, that's the worst disease of love,
The poore, the foule, the false, love can
Admit, but not the busied man.
He which hath businesse, and makes love, doth doe
Such wrong, as when a maryed man doth wooe.

THE ANNIVERSARIE

ALL Kings, and all their favorites,
　　All glory of honors, beauties, wits,
The Sun it selfe, which makes times, as they passe,
Is elder by a yeare, now, than it was
When thou and I first one another saw:
All other things, to their destruction draw,
　　Only our love hath no decay;
This, no to morrow hath, nor yesterday,
Running it never runs from us away,
But truly keepes, his first, last, everlasting day.

　　Two graves must hide thine and my coarse.
　　If one might, death were no divorce
Alas, as well as other Princes, wee,
(Who Prince enough in one another bee,)
Must leave at last in death, these eyes, and eares,
Oft fed with true oathes, and with sweet salt teares;
　　But soules where nothing dwells but love
(All other thoughts being inmates) then shall prove
This, or a love increased there above,
When bodies to their graves, soules from their
　　　graves remove.

　　And then wee shall be throughly blest,
　　But wee no more, than all the rest;
Here upon earth, we'are Kings, and none but wee
Can be such Kings, nor of such subjects bee.
Who is so safe as wee? where none can doe
Treason to us, except one of us two.
　　True and false feares let us refraine,
Let us love nobly, and live, and adde againe
Yeares and yeares unto yeares, till we attaine
To write threescore: this is the second of our raigne.

A VALEDICTION: OF MY NAME,
IN THE WINDOW

I

My name engrav'd herein,
Doth contribute my firmnesse to this glasse.
  Which, ever since that charme, hath beene
  As hard, as that which grav'd it, was;
Thine eye will give it price enough, to mock
    The diamonds of either rock.

II

    'Tis much that glasse should bee
As all confessing, and through-shine as I,
  'Tis more, that it shewes thee to thee,
  And cleare reflects thee to thine eye.
But all such rules, loves magique can undoe
    Here you see mee, and I am you.

III

    As no one point, nor dash,
Which are but accessaries to this name,
  The showers and tempests can outwash,
  So shall all times finde mee the same;
You this intirenesse better may fulfill,
    Who have the patterne with you still.

IIII

    Or if too hard and deepe
This learning be, for a scratch'd name to teach,
  It, as a given deaths head keepe,

Lovers mortalitie to preach,
Or thinke this ragged bony name to bee
My ruinous Anatomie.

V

Then, as all my soules bee,
Emparadis'd in you, (in whom alone
I understand, and grow and see,)
The rafters of my body, bone
Being still with you, the Muscle, Sinew, and Veine,
Which tile this house, will come againe.

VI

Till my returne, repaire
And recompact my scattered body so.
As all the vertuous powers which are
Fix'd in the starres, are said to flow
Into such characters, as graved bee
When these starres have supremacie:

VII

So since this name was cut
When love and griefe their exaltation had,
No doore 'gainst this names influence shut
As much more loving, as more sad,
'Twill make thee; and thou shouldst, till I returne,
Since I die daily, daily mourne.

VIII

When thy inconsiderate hand
Flings ope this casement, with my trembling name,
To looke on one, whose wit or land,
New battry to thy heart may frame,
Then thinke this name alive, and that thou thus
In it offendst my Genius,

IX

And when thy melted maid,
Corrupted by thy Lover's gold, and page,
His letter at thy pillow'hath laid,
Disputed it, and tam'd thy rage,
And thou begin'st to thaw towards him, for this,
May my name step in, and hide his.

x

And if this treason goe
To an overt act, and that thou write againe;
In superscribing, this name flow
Into thy fancy from the pane.
So, in forgetting thou remembrest right,
And unaware to mee shalt write.

XI

But glasse, and lines must bee,
No meanes our firme substantiall love to keepe
Neere death inflicts this lethargie,
And this I murmure in my sleepe;
Impute this idle talke, to that I goe,
For dying men talke often so.

TWICKNAM GARDEN

Blasted with sighs, and surrounded with teares,
Hither I come to seeke the spring,
And at mine eyes, and at mine eares,
Receive such balmes, as else cure every thing;
But O, selfe traytor, I do bring
The spider love, which transubstantiates all,

And can convert Manna to gall,
And that this place may thoroughly be thought
  True Paradise, I have the serpent brought.

'Twere wholsomer for mee, that winter did
  Benight the glory of this place,
  And that a grave frost did forbid
These trees to laugh, and mocke mee to my face;
  But that I may not this disgrace
Indure, nor yet leave loving, Love let mee
  Some senslesse peece of this place bee:
Make me a mandrake, so I may groane here,
  Or a stone fountaine weeping out my yeare.

Hither with christall vyals, lovers come,
  And take my teares, which are loves wine,
  And try your mistresse Teares at home,
For all are false, that tast not just like mine;
  Alas, hearts do not in eyes shine,
Nor can you more judge womans thoughts by teares.
  Than by her shadow, what she weares.
O perverse sexe, where none is true but shee,
  Who's therefore true, because her truth kills mee.

A VALEDICTION: OF THE BOOKE

I'LL tell thee now (deare Love) what thou shalt doe
  To anger destiny, as she doth us,
  How I shall stay, though she Esloygne me thus
And how posterity shall know it too;
    How thine may out-endure
    Sybills glory, and obscure
    Her who from Pindar could allure,
  And her, through whose helpe *Lucan* is not lame,
And her, whose booke (they say) *Homer* did finde,
      and name.

Study our manuscripts, those Myriades
    Of letters, which have past twixt thee and mee,
    Thence write our Annals, and in them will bee
To all whom loves subliming fire invades,
        Rule and example found;
        There, the faith of any ground
        No schismatique will dare to wound,
    That sees, how Love this grace to us affords,
To make, to keep, to use, to be these his Records.

This Booke, as long-liv'd as the elements,
    Or as the worlds forme, this all-graved tome
    In cypher writ, or new made Idiome,
Wee for loves clergie only'are instruments:
        When this booke is made thus,
        Should againe the ravenous
        Vandals and Goths inundate us,
    Learning were safe; in this our Universe
Schooles might learne Sciences, Spheares Musick,
        Angels Verse.

Here Loves Divines, (since all Divinity
    Is love or wonder) may finde all they seeke,
    Whether abstract spirituall love they like,
Their Soules exhal'd with what they do not see,
        Or, loth so to amuze
        Faiths infirmitie, they chuse
        Something which they may see and use;
    For, though minde be the heaven, where love doth
        sit,
Beauty a convenient type may be to figure it.

Here more than in their bookes may Lawyers finde,
    Both by what titles Mistresses are ours,
    And how prerogative these states devours,
Transferr'd from Love himselfe, to womankinde,
        Who though from heart, and eyes,

They exact great subsidies,
   Forsake him who on them relies,
  And for the cause, honour, or conscience give,
Chimeraes, vaine as they, or their prerogative.

Here Statesmen, (or of them, they which can reade,)
   May of their occupation finde the grounds:
   Love and their art alike it deadly wounds,
If to consider what 'tis, one proceed,
     In both they doe excell
     Who the present governe well,
     Whose weaknesse none doth, or dares tell;
  In this thy booke, such will their nothing see,
As in the Bible some can finde out Alchimy.

Thus vent thy thoughts; abroad I'll studie thee,
   As he removes farre off, that great heights takes:
   How great love is, presence best tryall makes,
But absence tryes how long this love will bee;
     To take a latitude
     Sun, or starres, are fitliest view'd
     At their brightest, but to conclude
  Of longitudes, what other way have wee,
But to marke when, and where the darke eclipses
    bee?

LOVES GROWTH

I scarce beleeve my love to be so pure
As I had thought it was,
Because it doth endure
Vicissitude, and season, as the grasse;
Me thinkes I lyed all winter, when I swore,
My love was infinite, if spring make'it more.
But if this medicine, love, which cures all sorrow
With more, not onely bee no quintessence,

But mixt of all stuffes, paining soule, or sense,
And of the Sunne his working vigour borrow,
Love's not so pure, and abstract, as they use
To say, which have no Mistresse but their Muse,
But as all else, being elemented too,
Love sometimes would contemplate, sometimes do.

And yet no greater, but more eminent,
    Love by the Spring is growne;
      As, in the firmament,
Starres by the Sunne are not inlarg'd, but showne.
Gentle love deeds, as blossomes on a bough,
From loves awakened root do bud out now.
If. as in water stir'd more circles bee
Produc'd by one, love such additions take,
Those like so many spheares, but one heaven make,
For, they are all concentrique unto thee.
And though each spring doe adde to love new heate,
As princes doe in times of action get
New taxes, and remit them not in peace,
No winter shall abate the springs encrease.

LOVES EXCHANGE

    Love, any devill else but you,
    Would for a given Soule give something too.
    At Court your fellowes every day,
    Give th'art of Riming, Huntsmanship, or Play,
    For them which were their owne before;
    Onely I have nothing which gave more,
    But am, alas, by being lowly, lower.

    I aske no dispensation now
    To falsifie a teare, or sigh, or vow,
    I do not sue from thee to draw

A *non obstante* on natures law,
These are prerogatives, they inhere
In thee and thine; none should forsweare
Except that hee *Loves* minion were.

Give mee thy weaknesse, make mee blinde,
Both wayes, as thou and thine, in eies and minde;
Love, let me never know that this
Is love, or, that love childish is.
Let me not know that others know
That she knowes my paines, lest that so
A tender shame make me mine owne new woe.

If thou give nothing, yet thou'art just,
Because I would not thy first motions trust;
Small townes which stand stiffe, till great shot
Enforce them, by warres law *condition* not.
Such in loves warfare is my case,
I may not article for grace,
Having put Love at last to shew this face.

This face, by which he could command
And change the Idolatrie of any land,
This face, which wheresoe'r it comes,
Can .call vow'd men from cloisters, dead from
        tombes,
And melt both Poles at once, and store
Deserts with cities, and make more
Mynes in the earth, than Quarries were before.

For this, Love is enrag'd with mee,
Yet kills not. If I must example bee
To future Rebells; If th'unborne
Must learne, by my being cut up, and torne:
Kill, and dissect me, Love; for this
Torture against thine owne end is,
Rack't carcasses make ill Anatomies.

THE DREAME

DEARE love, for nothing lesse than thee
Would I have broke this happy dreame,
      It was a theame
For reason, much too strong for phantasie,
Therefore thou wakd'st me wisely; yet
My Dreame thou brok'st not, but continued'st it,
Thou art so truth, that thoughts of thee suffice,
To make dreames truths; and fables histories;
Enter these armes, for since thou thoughtst it best,
Not to dreame all my dreame, let's act the rest.

As lightning, or a Tapers light,
Thine eyes, and not thy noise wak'd mee;
      Yet I thought thee
(For thou lovest truth) an Angell, at first sight,
But when I saw thou sawest my heart,
And knew'st my thoughts, beyond an Angels art,
When thou knew'st what I dreamt, when thou knew'st
    when
Excesse of joy would wake me, and cam'st then,
I must confesse, it could not chuse but bee
Prophane, to thinke thee any thing but thee.

Comming and staying show'd thee, thee,
But rising makes me doubt, that now,
      Thou art not thou.
That love is weake, where feare's as strong as hee;
'Tis not all spirit, pure, and brave,
If mixture it of *Feare, Shame, Honor,* have.
Perchance as torches which must ready bee,
Men light and put out, so thou deal'st with mee,
Thou cam'st to kindle, goest to come; Then I
Will dreame that hope againe, but else would die.

A VALEDICTION: OF WEEPING

LET me powre forth
My teares before thy face, whil'st I stay here,
For thy face coines them, and thy stampe they beare,
And by this Mintage they are something worth,
      For thus they bee
      Pregnant of thee;
Fruits of much griefe they are, emblemes of more,
When a teare falls, that thou falls which it bore,
So thou and I are nothing then, when on a divers shore.

      On a round ball
A workeman that hath copies by, can lay
An Europe, Afrique, and an Asia,
And quickly make that, which was nothing, *All*:
      So doth each teare,
      Which thee doth weare,
A globe, yea world by that impression grow,
Till thy teares mixt with mine doe overflow
This world, by waters sent from thee, my heaven
    dissolved so.

      O more than Moone,
Draw not up seas to drowne me in thy spheare,
Weepe me not dead, in thine armes, but forbeare
To teach the sea, what it may doe too soone;
      Let not the winde
      Example finde,
To doe me more harme, than it purposeth;
Since thou and I sigh one anothers breath,
Who e'r sighes most, is cruellest, and hastes the others
    death.

LOVES ALCHYMIE

SOME that have deeper digg'd loves Myne than I,
Say, where his centrique happinesse doth lie:
  I have lov'd, and got, and told,
But should I love, get, tell, till I were old,
I should not finde that hidden mysterie;
  Oh, 'tis imposture all:
And as no chymique yet th'Elixar got,
  But glorifies his pregnant pot,
  If by the way to him befall
Some odoriferous thing, or medicinall,
  So, lovers dreame a rich and long delight,
  But get a winter-seeming summers night.

Our ease, our thrift, our honour, and our day,
Shall we, for this vaine Bubles shadow pay?
  Ends love in this, that my man,
Can be as happy'as I can; If he can
Endure the short scorne of a Bridegroomes play?
  That loving wretch that sweares,
'Tis not the bodies marry, but the mindes,
  Which he in her Angelique findes,
  Would sweare as justly, that he heares,
In that dayes rude hoarse minstralsey, the spheares.
Hope not for minde in women; at their best
Sweetnesse and wit, they'are but *Mummy*, possest.

THE FLEA

MARKE but this flea, and marke in this,
How little that which thou deny'st me is;
It suck'd me first, and now sucks thee,
And in this flea, our two bloods mingled bee;

Thou know'st that this cannot be said
A sinne, nor shame, nor losse of maidenhead,
   Yet this enjoyes before it wooe,
     And pamper'd swells with one blood made of two
     And this, alas, is more than wee would doe.

Oh stay, three lives in one flea spare,
Where wee almost, yea more than maryed are.
This flea is you and I, and this
Our mariage bed, and mariage temple is;
Though parents grudge, and you, w'are met,
And cloysterd in these living walls of Jet.
   Though use make you apt to kill mee,
     Let not to that, selfe murder added bee,
     And sacrilege, three sinnes in killing three.

Cruell and sodaine, hast thou since
Purpled thy naile, in blood of innocence?
Wherein could this flea guilty bee,
Except in that drop which it suckt from thee?
Yet thou triumph'st, and saist that thou
Find'st not thy selfe, nor mee the weaker now;
   'Tis true, then learne how false, feares bee;
     Just so much honor, when thou yeeld'st to mee,
     Will wast, as this flea's death tooke life from thee.

THE CURSE

Who ever guesses, thinks, or dreames he knowes
Who is my mistris, wither by this curse;
     His only, and only his purse
     May some dull heart to love dispose,
And shee yeeld then to all that are his foes;
   May he be scorn'd by one, whom all else scorne,
   Forsweare to others, what to her he'hath sworne,
   With feare of missing, shame of getting, torne:

Madnesse his sorrow, gout his cramp, may hee
Make, by but thinking, who hath made him such:
    And may he feele no touch
    Of conscience, but of fame, and bee
Anguish'd, not that'twas sinne, but that'twas shee:
    In early and long scarcenesse may he rot,
    For land which had been his, if he had not
    Himselfe incestuously an heire begot:

May he dreame Treason, and beleeve, that hee
Meant to performe it, and confesse, and die,
    And no record tell why:
    His sonnes, which none of his may bee,
Inherite nothing but his infamie:
    Or may he so long Parasites have fed,
    That he would faine be theirs, whom he hath bred
    And at the last be circumcis'd for bread:

The venom of all stepdames, gamsters gall,
What Tyrans, and their subjects interwish,
    What Plants, Myne, Beasts, Foule, Fish,
    Can contribute, all ill which all
Prophets, or Poets spake; And all which shall
    Be annex'd in schedules unto this by mee,
    Fall on that man; For if it be a shee
    Nature beforehand hath out-cursed mee.

THE MESSAGE

SEND home my long strayd eyes to mee,
Which (Oh) too long have dwelt on thee;
Yet since there they have learn'd such ill,
        Such forc'd fashions,
        And false passions,
            That they be
            Made by thee
Fit for no good sight, keep them still.

Send home my harmlesse heart againe,
Which no unworthy thought could staine;
But if it be taught by thine
　　　To make jestings
　　　Of protestings,
　　　　　And crosse both
　　　　　Word and oath,
Keepe it, for then 'tis none of mine.

Yet send me back my heart and eyes,
That I may know, and see thy lyes,
And may laugh and joy, when thou
　　　Art in anguish
　　　And dost languish
　　　　　For some one
　　　　　That will none,
Or prove as false as thou art now.

A NOCTURNALL UPONS. LUCIES DAY.

BEING THE SHORTEST DAY

Tis the yeares midnight, and it is the dayes,
Lucies, who scarce seaven houres herself unmaskes,
　The Sunne is spent, and now his flasks
　Send forth light squibs, no constant rayes;
　　The worlds whole sap is sunke:
The generall balme th'hydroptique earth hath drunk.
Whither, as to the beds-feet, life is shrunke,
Dead and enterr'd; yet all these seeme to laugh,
Compar'd with mee, who am their Epitaph.

Study me then, you who shall lovers bee
At the next world, that is, at the next Spring:
　For I am every dead thing,

In whom love wrought new Alchimie.
 For his art did expresse
A quintessence even from nothingnesse,
From dull privations, and leane emptinesse:
He ruin'd mee, and I am re-begot
Of absence, darknesse, death; things which are not.

All others, from all things, draw all that's good,
Life, soule, forme, spirit, whence they beeing have;
 I, by loves limbecke, am the grave
 Of all, that's nothing. Oft a flood
  Have'wee two wept, and so
Drownd the whole world, us two; oft did we grow
To be two Chaosses, when we did show
Care to ought else; and often absences
Withdrew our soules, and made us carcasses.

But I am by her death, (which word wrongs her)
Of the first nothing, the Elixer grown;
 Were I a man, that I were one,
 I needs must know; I should preferre,
  If I were any beast,
Some ends, some means; Yea plants, yea stones detest,
And love; All, all some properties invest;
If I an ordinary nothing were,
As shadow, a light, and body must be here.

But I am None; nor will my Sunne renew.
You lovers, for whose sake, the lesser Sunne
 At this time to the Goat is runne
 To fetch new lust, and give it you,
  Enjoy your summer all;
Since shee enjoyes her long nights festivall,
Let mee prepare towards her, and let mee call
This houre her Vigill, and her Eve, since this
Both the yeares, and the dayes deep midnight is.

WITCHCRAFT BY A PICTURE

I FIXE mine eye on thine, and there
   Pitty my picture burning in thine eye,
My picture drown'd in a transparent teare,
   When I looke lower I espie;
     Hadst thou the wicked skill
By pictures made and mard, to kill,
How many wayes mightst thou performe thy will?

But now I have drunke thy sweet salt teares,
   And though thou poure more I'll depart;
My picture vanish'd, vanish feares,
   That I can be endamag'd by that art;
     Though thou retaine of mee
One picture more, yet that will bee,
Being in thine owne heart, from all malice free.

THE BAITE

COME live with mee, and bee my love,
And wee will some new pleasures prove
Of golden sands, and christall brookes,
With silken lines, and silver hookes.

There will the river whispering runne
Warm'd by thy eyes, more than the Sunne.
And there the'inamor'd fish will stay,
Begging themselves they may betray.

When thou wilt swimme in that live bath,
Each fish, which every channell hath,
Will amorously to thee swimme,
Gladder to catch thee, than thou him.

If thou, to be so seene, beest loath,
By Sunne, or Moone, thou darknest both,
And if my selfe have leave to see,
I need not their light, having thee.

Let others freeze with angling reeds,
And cut their legges, with shells and weeds,
Or treacherously poore fish beset,
With strangling snare, or windowie net:

Let coarse bold hands, from slimy nest
The bedded fish in banks out-wrest,
Or curious traitors, sleavesilke flies
Bewitch poore fishes wandring eyes.

For thee, thou needst no such deceit,
For thou thy selfe art thine owne bait;
That fish, that is not catch'd thereby,
Alas, is wiser farre than I.

THE APPARITION

When by thy scorne, O murdresse, I am dead,
And that thou thinkst thee free
From all solicitation from mee,
Then shall my ghost come to thy bed,
And thee, fain'd vestall, in worse armes shall see;
Then thy sicke taper will begin to winke,
And he, whose thou art then, being tyr'd before,
Will, if thou stirre, or pinch to wake him, thinke
    Thou call'st for more,
And in false sleepe will from thee shrinke,
And then poore Aspen wretch, neglected thou
Bath'd in a cold quicksilver sweat wilt lye
    A veryer ghost than I;

What I will say, I will not tell thee now,
Lest that preserve thee'; and since my love is spent,
I'had rather thou shouldst painfully repent,
Than by my threatnings rest still innocent.

THE BROKEN HEART

He is starke mad, who ever sayes,
   That he hath been in love an houre,
Yet not that love so soone decayes,
   But that it can tenne in lesse space devour;
Who will beleeve mee, if I sweare
That I have had the plague a yeare?
     Who would not laugh at mee, if I should say,
     I saw a flaske of *powder burne a day?*

Ah, what a trifle is a heart,
   If once into loves hands it come!
All other griefes allow a part
   To other griefes, and aske themselves but some;
They come to us, but us Love draws,
Hee swallows us, and never chawes:
     By him, as by chain'd shot, whole rankes doe
       dye,
     He is the tyran Pike, our hearts the Frye.

If 'twere not so, what did become
   Of my heart, when I first saw thee?
I brought a heart into the roome,
   But from the roome, I carried none with mee:
If it had gone to thee, I know
Mine would have taught thine heart to show
     More pitty unto mee: but Love, alas,
     At one first blow did shiver it as glasse.

Yet nothing can to nothing fall,
  Nor any place be empty quite,
Therefore I thinke my breast hath all
  Those peeces still, though they be not unite;
And now as broken glasses show
A hundred lesser faces, so
    My ragges of heart can like, wish, and adore,
    But after one such love, can love no more.

A VALEDICTION: FORBIDDING MOURNING

As virtuous men passe mildly away,
  And whisper to their soules, to goe,
Whilst some of their sad friends doe say,
  The breath goes now, and some say, no:

So let us melt, and make no noise,
  No teare-floods, nor sigh-tempests move,
T'were prophanation of our joyes
  To tell the layetie our love.

Moving of th'earth brings harmes and feares,
  Men reckon what it did and meant,
But trepidation of the spheares,
  Though greater farre, is innocent.

Dull sublunary lovers love
  (Whose soule is sense) cannot admit
Absence, because it doth remove
  Those things which elemented it.

But we by a love, so much refin'd,
  That our selves know not what it is,
Inter-assured of the mind,
  Care lesse, eyes, lips, and hands to misse

Our two soules therefore, which are one,
  Though I must goe, endure not yet
A breaoh, but an expansion,
  Like gold to ayery thinnesse beate.

If they be two, they are two so
  As stiffe twin compasses are two,
Thy soule the fixt foot, makes no show
  To move, but doth, if the'other doe.

And though it in the center sit,
  Yet when the other far doth rome,
It leanes, and hearkens after it,
  And growes erect, as that comes home.

Such wilt thou be to mee, who must
  Like th'other foot, obliquely runne;
Thy firmnes drawes my circle just,
  And makes me end, where I begunne.

THE EXTASIE

WHERE, like a pillow on a bed,
  A Pregnant banke swel'd up, to rest
The violets reclining head,
  Sat we two, one anothers best.
Our hands were firmely cimented
  With a fast balme, which thence did spring,
Our eye-beames twisted, and did thred
  Our eyes, upon one double string;
So to'entergraft our hands, as yet
  Was all the meanes to make us one,
And pictures in our eyes to get
  Was all our propagation.
As 'twixt two equall Armies, Fate

Suspends uncertaine victorie,
  Our soules, (which to advance their state,
    Were gone out,) hung 'twixt her, and mee.
And whil'st our soules negotiate there,
    Wee like sepulchrall statues lay;
All day, the same our postures were,
    And wee said nothing, all the day.
If any, so by love refin'd,
    That he soules language understood,
And by good love were growen all minde,
    Within convenient distance stood,
He (though he knew not which soul spake,
    Because both meant, both spake the same)
Might thence a new concoction take,
    And part farre purer than he came.
This Extasie doth unperplex
    (We said) and tell us what we love,
Wee see by this, it was not sexe,
    Wee see, we saw not what did move:
But as all severall soules containe
    Mixture of things, they know not what,
Love, these mixt soules, doth mixe againe,
    And makes both one, each this and that.
A single violet transplant,
    The strength, the colour, and the size,
(All which before was poore, and scant,)
    Redoubles still, and multiplies.
When love, with one another so
    Interinanimates two soules,
That abler soule, which thence doth flow,
    Defects of lonelinesse controules.
Wee then, who are this new soule, know,
    Of what we are compos'd, and made,
For, th'Atomies of which we grow,
    Are soules, whom no change can invade.
But O alas, so long, so farre
    Our bodies why doe wee forbeare?

They are ours, though they are not wee, Wee are
   The intelligences, they the spheares.
We owe them thankes, because they thus,
   Did us, to us, at first convay,
Yeelded their forces, sense, to us,
   Nor are drosse to us, but allay.
On man heavens influence workes not so,
   But that it first imprints the ayre,
Soe soule into the soule may flow,
   Though it to body first repaire.
As our blood labours to beget
   Spirits, as like soules as it can,
Because such fingers need to knit
   That subtile knot, which makes us man:
So must pure lovers soules descend
   T'affections, and to faculties,
Which sense may reach and apprehend,
   Else a great Prince in prison lies.
To'our bodies turne wee then, that so
   Weake men on love reveal'd may looke;
Loves mysteries in soules doe grow,
   But yet the body is his booke.
And if some lover, such as wee,
   Have heard this dialogue of one,
Let him still marke us, he shall see
   Small change, when we'are to bodies gone

LOVES DEITIE

I LONG to talke with some old lovers ghost,
   Who dyed before the god of Love was borne:
I cannot thinke that hee, who then lov'd most,
   Sunke so low, as to love one which did scorne.
But since this god produc'd a destinie,
And that vice-nature, custome, lets it be;
   I must love her, that loves not mee.

Sure, they which made him god, meant not so much
    Nor he, in his young godhead practis'd it.
But when an even flame two hearts did touch,
    His office was indulgently to fit
Actives to passives. Correspondencie
Only his subject was; It cannot bee
    Love, till I love her, that loves mee.

But every moderne god will now extend
    His vast prerogative, as far as Jove.
To rage, to lust, to write to, to commend,
    All is the purlewe of the God of Love.
Oh were wee wak'ned by this Tyrannie
To ungod this child againe, it could not bee
    I should love her, who loves not mee.

Rebell and Atheist too, why murmure I,
    As though I felt the worst that love could doe?
Love might make me leave loving, or might trie
    A deeper plague, to make her love mee too,
Which, since she loves before, I'am loth to see;
Falshood is worse than hate; and that must bee,
    If shee whom I love, should love mee.

THE FUNERALL

Who ever comes to shroud me, do not harme
        Nor question much
That subtile wreath of haire, which crowns my arme;
The mystery, the signe you must not touch,
        For'tis my outward Soule,
Viceroy to that, which then to heaven being gone,
        Will leave this to controule,
And keep these limbes, her Provinces, from dissolution.

For if the sinewie thread my braine lets fall
      Through every part,
Can tye those parts, and make mee one of all;
These haires which upward grew, and strength and art
      Have from a better braine,
Can better do'it; Except she meant that I
      By this should know my pain,
As prisoners then are manacled, when they'are
      condemn'd to die.

What ere shee meant by'it, bury it with me,
      For since I am
Loves martyr, it might breed idolatrie,
If into others hands these Reliques came;
      As'twas humility
To afford to it all that a Soule can doe,
      So,'tis some bravery,
That since you would save none of mee, I bury some of
      you.

THE BLOSSOME

    LITTLE think'st thou, poore flower,
      Whom I have watch'd sixe or seaven dayes,
And seene thy birth, and seene what every houre
Gave to thy growth, thee to this height to raise,
And now dost laugh and triumph on this bough,
      Little think'st thou
That it will freeze anon, and that I shall
To morrow finde thee falne, or not at all.

    Little think'st thou poore heart
      That labour'st yet to nestle thee,
And think'st by hovering here to get a part
In a forbidden or forbidding tree,
And hop'st her stiffenesse by long siege to bow:

Little think'st thou,
That thou to morrow, ere that Sunne doth wake,
Must with this Sunne, and mee a journey take.

But thou which lov'st to bee
Subtile to plague thy selfe, wilt say,
Alas, if you must goe, what's that to mee?
Here lyes my businesse, and here I will stay:
You goe to friends, whose love and meanes present
Various content
To your eyes, eares, and tongue, and every part.
If then your body goe, what need you a heart?

Well then, stay here; but know,
When thou hast stayd and done thy most;
A naked thinking heart, that makes no show,
Is to a woman, but a kinde of Ghost;
How shall shee know my heart; or having none,
Know thee for one?
Practise may make her know some other part,
But take my word, shee doth not know a Heart.

Meet mee at London, then,
Twenty dayes hence, and thou shalt see
Mee fresher and more fat, by being with men,
Than if I had staid still with her and thee.
For Gods sake, if you can, be you so too:
I would give you
There, to another friend, whom wee shall finde
As glad to have my body, as my minde

THE RELIQUE

WHEN my grave is broke up againe
Some second ghest to entertaine,
(For graves have learn'd that woman-head

To be to more than one a Bed)
          And he that digs it, spies
A bracelet of bright haire about the bone,
          Will he not let'us alone,
And thinke that there a loving couple lies,
Who thought that this device might be some way
To make their soules, at the last busie day,
Meet at this grave, and make a little stay?

          If this fall in a time, or land,
          Where mis-devotion doth command,
          Then, he that digges us up, will bring
          Us, to the Bishop, and the King,
          To make us Reliques; then
Thou shalt be a Mary Magdalen, and I
          A something else thereby;
All women shall adore us, and some men;
And since at such time, miracles are sought,
I would have that age by this paper taught
What miracles wee harmlesse lovers wrought.

          First, we lov'd well and faithfully,
          Yet knew not what wee lov'd, nor why,
          Difference of sex no more wee knew,
          Than our Guardian Angells doe;
          Comming and going, wee
Perchance might kisse, but not between those meales;
          Our hands ne'r toucht the seales,
Which nature, injur'd by late law, sets free:
These miracles wee did; but now alas,
All measure, and all language, I should passe,
Should I tell what a miracle shee was.

THE DAMPE

WHEN I am dead, and Doctors know not why,
    And my friends curiositie
Will have me cut up to survay each part,
When they shall finde your Picture in my heart,
    You thinke a sodaine dampe of love
    Will through all their senses move,
And worke on them as mee, and so preferre
Your murder, to the name of Massacre.

Poore victories! But if you dare be brave,
    And pleasure in your conquest have,
First kill th'enormous Gyant, your *Disdaine*,
And let th'enchantresse *Honor*, next be slaine,
    And like a Goth and Vandall rize,
    Deface Records, and Histories
Of your owne arts and triumphs over men,
And without such advantage kill me then.

For I could muster up as well as you
    My Gyants, and my Witches too,
Which are vast *Constancy*, and *Secretnesse*,
But these I neyther looke for, nor professe;
    Kill mee as Woman, let mee die
    As a meere man; doe you but try
Your passive valor, and you shall finde then,
Naked you'have odds enough of any man.

A JEAT RING SENT

THOU art not so black, as my heart,
Nor halfe so brittle, as her heart, thou art;
What would'st thou say? shall both our properties by
    thee bee spoke,
    Nothing more endlesse, nothing sooner broke?

Marriage rings are not of this stuffe;
  Oh, why should ought lesse precious, or lesse tough
Figure our loves? Except in thy name thou have bid it
      say,
  I'am cheap, and nought but fashion, fling me'away.

Yet stay with mee since thou art come,
  Circle this fingers top, which did'st her thombe.
Be justly proud, and gladly safe, that thou dost dwell
      with me,
  She that, Oh, broke her faith, would soon breake thee.

THE PROHIBITION

Take heed of loving mee,
At least remember, I forbade it thee;
Not that I shall repaire my'unthrifty wast
Of Breath and Blood, upon thy sighes, and teares,
By being to thee then what to me thou wast;
But, so great Joy, our life at once outweares,
Then, lest thy love, by my death, frustrate bee,
If thou love mee, take heed of loving mee.

Take heed of hating mee,
Or too much triumph in the Victorie.
Not that I shall be mine owne officer,
And hate with hate againe retaliate;
But thou wilt lose the stile of conquerour,
If I, thy conquest, perish by thy hate.
Then, lest my being nothing lessen thee,
If thou hate mee, take heed of hating mee.

Yet, love and hate mee too,
So, these extreames shall neithers office doe;
Love mee, that I may die the gentler way;

Hate mee, because thy love is too great for mee;
Or let these two, themselves, not me decay;
So shall I, live, thy Stage, not triumph bee;
Lest thou thy love and hate and mee undoe,
To let mee live, O love and hate mee too.

THE EXPIRATION

So, so, breake off this last lamenting kisse,
   Which sucks two soules, and vapors Both away,
Turne thou ghost that way, and let mee turne this,
   And let our selves benight our happiest day,
We ask'd none leave to love; nor will we owe
   Any, so cheape a death, as saying, Goe;

Goe; and if that word have not quite kil'd thee,
   Ease mee with death, by bidding mee goe too.
Oh, if it have, let my word worke on mee,
   And a just office on a murderer doe.
Except it be too late, to kill me so,
   Being double dead, going, and bidding, goe.

THE COMPUTATION

For the first twenty yeares, since yesterday,
   I scarce beleev'd, thou could'st be gone away,
For forty more, I fed on favours past,
   And forty'on hopes, that thou would'st, they might
      last.
Teares drown'd one hundred, and sighes blew out two,
   A thousand, I did neither thinke, nor doe,
   Or not divide, all being one thought of you;
   Or in a thousand more, forgot that too.
Yet call not this long life; But thinke that I
Am, by being dead, Immortall; Can ghosts die?

THE PARADOX

No Lover saith, I love, nor any other
    Can judge a perfect Lover;
Hee thinkes that else none can, nor will agree
    That any loves but hee:
I cannot say I lov'd, for who can say
    Hee was kill'd yesterday?
Love with excesse of heat, more yong than old,
    Death kills with too much cold;
Wee dye but once, and who lov'd last did die,
    Hee that saith twice, doth lye:
For though hee seeme to move, and stirre a while,
    If doth the sense beguile.
Such life is like the light which bideth yet
    When the lights life is set,
Or like the heat, which fire in solid matter
    Leaves behinde, two houres after.
Once I lov'd and dy'd; and am now become
    Mine Epitaph and Tombe.
Here dead men speake their last, and so do I;
    Love-slaine, loe, here I lye.

FAREWELL TO LOVE

    WHILST yet to prove,
I thought there was some Deitie in love
  So did I reverence, and gave
Worship; as Atheists at their dying houre
Call, what they cannot name, an unknowne power,
  As ignorantly did I crave:
        Thus when
Things not yet knowne are coveted by men,

Our desires give them fashion, and so
As they waxe lesser, fall, as they sise, grow.

But, from late faire
His highnesse sitting in a golden Chaire,
   Is not lesse cared for after three dayes
By children, than the thing which lovers so
Blindly admire, and with such worship wooe;
   Being had, enjoying it decayes:
            And thence,
What before pleas'd them all, takes but one sense,
   And that so lamely, as it leaves behinde
A kinde of sorrowing dulnesse to the minde.

Ah cannot wee,
As well as Cocks and Lyons jocund be,
   After such pleasures? Unlesse wise
Nature decreed (since each such Act, they say,
Diminisheth the length of life a day)
   This, as shee would man should despise
            The sport,
Because that other curse of being short,
   And onely for a minute made to be
Eagers desire, to raise posterity.

Since so, my minde
Shall not desire what no man else can finde,
   I'll no more dote and runne
To pursue things which had indammag'd me.
And when I come where moving beauties be,
   As men doe when the summers Sunne
            Growes great,
Though I admire their greatnesse, shun their heat;
   Each place can afford shadowes. If all faile,
'Tis but applying worme-seed to the Taile.

A LECTURE UPON THE SHADOW

STAND still, and I will read to thee
A Lecture, love, in Loves philosophy.
    These three houres that we have spent,
    Walking here, Two shadows went
Along with us, which we our selves produc'd;
But, now the Sunne is just above our head,
    We doe those shadowes tread;
    And to brave clearnesse all things are reduc'd.
    So whilst our infant loves did grow,
   Disguises did, and shadowes, flow,
   From us, and our cares; but, now 'tis not so.

That love hath not attain'd the high'st degree,
Which is still diligent lest others see.

Except our loves at this noone stay,
We shall new shadowes make the other way.
    As the first were made to blinde
    Others; these which come behinde
Will worke upon our selves, and blind our eyes
If our loves faint, and westwardly decline;
    To me thou, falsly, thine,
    And I to thee mine actions shall disguise.
   The morning shadowes weare away,
   But these grow longer all the day,
   But oh, loves day is short, if love decay.

Love is a growing, or full constant light;
And his first minute, after noone, is night.

SONNET. THE TOKEN

Send me some token, that my hope may live,
   Or that my easelesse thou ghts may sleep and rest;
Send me some honey to make sweet my hive,
   That in my passion I may hope the best.
I beg noe ribbond wrought with thine owne hands,
    To knit our loves in the fantastick straine
Of new-toucht youth; nor Ring to shew the stands
   Of our affection, that as that's round and plaine,
So should our loves meet in simplicity.
   No, nor the Coralls which thy wrist infold,
Lac'd up together in congruity,
   To shew our thoughts should rest in the same hold;
No, nor thy picture, though most gracious,
   And most desir'd, because best like the best;
Nor witty Lines, which are most copious,
   Within the Writings which thou hast addrest.

Send me nor this, nor that, t'increase my store,
But swear thou thinkst I love thee, and no more.

A BURNT SHIP

Out of a fired ship, which, by no way
But drowning, could be rescued from the flame,
Some men leap'd forth, and ever as they came
Neere the foes ships, did by their shot decay;
So all were lost, which in the ship were found,
    They in the sea being burnt, they in the burnt ship
        drown'd.

A LAME BEGGER

I am unable, yonder begger cries,
To stand, or move; if he say true, hee *lies*.

ANTIQUARY

If in his Studie he hath so much care
To'hang all old strange things, let his wife beware.

IV

THE PERFUME

Once, and but once found in thy company,
All thy suppos'd escapes are laid on mee;
And as a thiefe at barre, is question'd there
By all the men, that have beene rob'd that yeare,
So am I, (by this traiterous meanes surpriz'd)
By thy Hydroptique father catechiz'd.
Though he had wont to search with glazed eyes,
As though he came to kill a Cockatrice,
Though hee hath oft sworne, that hee would remove
Thy beauties beautie, and food of our love,
Hope of his goods, if I with thee were seene,
Yet close and secret, as our soules, we'have beene.
Though thy immortall mother which doth lye
Still buried in her bed, yet will not dye,
Takes this advantage to sleepe out day-light,
And watch thy entries, and returnes all night,
And, when she takes thy hand, and would seeme kind,
Doth search what rings, and armelets she can finde,
And kissing notes the colour of thy face,
And fearing least thou'art swolne, doth thee embrace;
To trie if thou long, doth name strange meates,
And notes thy palenesse, blushing, sighs, and sweats;
And politiquely will to thee confesse
The sinnes of her owne youths ranke lustinesse;
Yet love these Sorceries did remove, and move
Thee to gull thine owne mother for my love.
Thy little brethren, which like Faiery Sprights
Oft skipt into our chamber, those sweet nights,
And kist, and ingled on thy fathers knee,

Were brib'd next day, to tell what they did see:
The grim eight-foot-high iron-bound serving-man,
That oft names God in oathes, and onely then,
He that to barre the first gate, doth as wide
As the great Rhodian Colossus stride,
Which, if in hell no other paines there were,
Makes mee feare hell, because he must be there:
Though by thy father he were hir'd to this,
Could never witnesse any touch or kisse.
But Oh, too common ill, I brought with mee
That, which betray'd mee to my enemie:
A loud perfume, which at my entrance cryed
Even at thy fathers nose, so were wee spied.
When, like a tyran King, that in his bed
Smelt gunpowder, the pale wretch shivered.
Had it beene some bad smell, he would have thought
That his owne feet, or breath, that smell had wrought.
But as wee in our Ile emprisoned,
Where cattell onely,'and diverse dogs are bred,
The pretious Unicornes, strange monsters call,
So thought he good, strange, that had none at all.
I taught my silkes, their whistling to forbeare,
Even my opprest shoes, dumbe and speechlesse were,
Onely, thou bitter sweet, whom I had laid
Next mee, mee traiterously hast betraid,
And unsuspected hast invisibly
At once fled unto him, and staid with mee.
Base excrement of earth, which dost confound
Sense, from distinguishing the sicke from sound;
By thee the seely Amorous sucks his death
By drawing in a leprous harlots breath;
By thee, the greatest staine to mans estate
Falls on us, to be call'd effeminate;
Though you be much lov'd in the Princes hall,
There, things that seeme, exceed substantiall.
Gods, when yee fum'd on altars, were pleas'd well,
Because you'were burnt, not that they lik'd your smell;

You'are loathsome all, being taken simply alone,
Shall wee love ill things joyn'd, and hate each one?
If you were good, your good doth soone decay;
And you are rare, that takes the good away.
All my perfumes, I give most willingly
To'embalme thy fathers corse; What? will hee die?

V

HIS PICTURE

HERE take my Picture; though I bid farewell,
Thine, in my heart, where my soule dwels, shall dwell.
'Tis like me now, but I dead, 'twill be more
When wee are shadowes both, than'twas before.
When weather-beaten I come backe; my hand,
Perhaps with rude cares torne, or Sun beams tann'd,
My face and brest of hairecloth, and my head
With cares rash sodaine stormes, being o'rspread,
My body'a sack of bones, broken within,
And powders blew staines scatter'd on my skinne;
If rivall fooles taxe thee to'have lov'd a man,
So foule, and course, as, Oh, I may seeme then,
This shall say what I was: and thou shalt say,
Doe his hurts reach mee? doth my worth decay?
Or doe they reach his judging minde, that hee
Should now love lesse, what hee did love to see?
That which in him was faire and delicate,
Was but the milke, which in loves childish state
Did nurse it: who now is growne strong enough
To feed on that, which to disus'd tasts seemes tough.

IX

THE AUTUMNALL

No *Spring*, nor *Summer* Beauty hath such grace,
  As I have seen in one *Autumnall* face.
Yong *Beauties* force our love, and that's a *Rape*,
  This doth but *counsaile*, yet you cannot scape.
ft'were a *shame* to love, here t'were no *shame*,
  Affection here takes *Reverences* name.
Were her first yeares the *Golden Age*; That's true,
  But now she's *gold* oft tried, and ever new.
That was her torrid and inflaming time,
  This is her tolerable *Tropique clyme*.
Faire eyes, who askes more heate than comes from
        hence,
  He in a fever wishes pestilence.
Call not these wrinkles, *graves*; If *graves* they were,
  They were *Loves graves*; for else he is no where.
Yet lies not Love *dead* here, but here doth sit
  Vow'd to this trench, like an *Anachorit*.
And here, till hers, which must be his *death*, come,
  He doth not digge a *Grave*, but build a *Tombe*.
Here dwells he, though he sojourne ev'ry where,
  In *Progresse*, yet his standing house is here.
Here, where still *Evening* is; not *noone*, nor *night*;
  Where no *voluptuousnesse*, yet all *delight*.
In all her words, unto all hearers fit,
  You may at *Revels*, you at *Counsaile*, sit.
This is loves timber, youth his under-wood;
  There he, as wine in *June*, enrages blood,
Which then comes seasonabliest, when our tast
  And appetite to other things, is past.
Xerxes strange *Lydian* love, the *Platane* tree,

Was lov'd for age, none being so large as shee,
Or else because, being yong, nature did blesse
　　Her youth with ages glory, *Barrennesse*.
If we love things long sought, *Age* is a thing
　　Which we are fifty yeares in compassing.
If transitory things, which soone decay,
　　Age must be lovelyest at the latest day.
But name not *Winter-faces*, whose skin's slacke;
　　Lanke, as an unthrifts purse; but a soules sacke;
Whose *Eyes* seeke light within, for all here's shade;
　　Whose *mouthes* are holes, rather worne out, than
　　　　made,
Whose every tooth to a severall place is gone,
　　To vexe their soules at *Resurrection*;
Name not these living *Deaths-heads* unto mee,
　　For these, not *Ancient*, but *Antique* be.
I hate extreames; yet I had rather stay
　　With *Tombs*, than *Cradles*, to weare out a day.
Since such loves naturall lation is, may still
　　My love descend, and journey downe the hill,
Not panting after growing beauties, so,
　　I shall ebbe out with them, who home-ward goe.

XII

HIS PARTING FROM HER

Since she must go, and I must mourn, come Night,
Environ me with darkness, whilst I write:
Shadow that hell unto me, which alone
I am to suffer when my Love is gone.
Alas the darkest Magick cannot do it,
Thou and greate Hell to boot are shadows to it.
Should *Cinthia* quit thee, *Venus*, and each starre,
It would not forme one thought dark as mine are.

I could lend thee obscureness now, and say,
Out of my self, There should be no more Day,
Such is already my felt want of sight,
Did not the fires within me force a light.
Oh Love, that fire and darkness should be mixt,
Or to thy Triumphs soe strange torments fixt!
Is't because thou thy self art blind, that wee
Thy Martyrs must no more each other see?
Or tak'st thou pride to break us on the wheel,
And view old Chaos in the Pains we feel?
Or have we left undone some mutual Rite,
Through holy fear, that merits thy despight?
No, no. The falt was mine, impute it to me,
Or rather to conspiring destinie,
Which (since I lov'd for forme before) decreed,
That I should suffer when I lov'd indeed:
And therefore now, sooner than I can say,
I saw the golden fruit, 'tis rapt away.
Or as I had watcht one drop in a vast stream,
And I left wealthy only in a dream.
Yet Love, thou'rt blinder than thy self in this,
To vex my Dove-like friend for my amiss:
And, where my own sad truth may expiate
Thy wrath, to make her fortune run my fate:
So blinded Justice doth, when Favorites fall,
Strike them, their house, their friends, their followers
    all.
Was't not enough that thou didst dart thy fires
Into our blouds, inflaming our desires,
And made'st us sigh and glow, and pant, and burn,
And then thy self into our flame did'st turn?
Was't not enough, that thou didst hazard us
To paths in love so dark, so dangerous:
And those so ambush'd round with houshold spies,
And over all, thy husbands towring eyes
That flam'd with oylie sweat of jealousie:
Yet went we not still on with Constancie?

Have we not kept our guards, like spie on spie?
Had correspondence whilst the foe stood by?
Stoln (more to sweeten them) our many blisses
Of meetings, conference, embracements, kisses?
Shadow'd with negligence our most respects?
Varied our language through all dialects,
Of becks, winks, looks, and often under-boards
Spoak dialogues with our feet far from our words?
Have we prov'd all these secrets of our Art,
Yea, thy pale inwards, and thy panting heart?
And, after all this passed Purgatory,
Must sad divorce make us the vulgar story?
First let our eyes be rivited quite through
Our turning brains, and both our lips grow to
Let our armes clasp like Ivy, and our fear
Freese us together, that we may stick here,
Till Fortune, that would rive us, with the deed,
Strain her eyes open, and it make them bleed.
For Love it cannot be, whom hitherto
I have accus'd, should such a mischief doe.
Oh Fortune, thou'rt not worth my least exclame,
And plague enough thou hast in thy own shame.
Do thy great worst, my friend and I have armes,
Though not against thy strokes, against thy harmes
Rend us in sunder, thou canst not divide
Our bodies so, but that our souls are ty'd,
And we can love by letters still and gifts,
And thoughts and dreams; Love never wanteth shifts.
I will not look upon the quickning Sun,
But straight her beauty to my sense shall run;
The ayre shall note her soft, the fire most pure;
Water suggest her clear, and the earth sure.
Time shall not lose our passages; the Spring
How fresh our love was in the beginning;
The Summer how it ripened in the eare;
And Autumn, what our golden harvests were.
The Winter I'll not think on to spite thee,

But count it a lost season, so shall shee.
And dearest Friend, since we must part, drown night
With hope of Day, burthens well born are light.
Though cold and darkness longer hang somewhere,
Yet *Phoebus* equally lights all the Sphere.
And what he cannot in like Portions pay,
The world enjoyes in Mass, and so we may.
Be then ever your self, and let no woe
Win on your health, your youth, your beauty: so
Declare your self base fortunes Enemy,
No less by your contempt than constancy:
That I may grow enamoured on your mind,
When my own thoughts I there reflected find.
For this to th'comfort of my Dear I vow,
My Deeds shall still be what my words are now;
The Poles shall move to teach me ere I start;
And when I change my Love, I'll change my heart;
Nay, if I wax but cold in my desire,
Think, heaven hath motion lost, and the world, fire:
Much more I could, but many words have made
That, oft, suspected which men would perswade;
Take therefore all in this: I love so true,
As I will never look for less in you.

XVI

ON HIS MISTRIS

By our first strange and fatall interview,
By all desires which thereof did ensue,
By our long starving hopes, by that remorse
Which my words masculine perswasive force
Begot in thee, and by the memory
Of hurts, which spies and rivals threatned me,
I calmly beg: But by thy fathers wrath,

By all paines, which want and divorcement hath,
I conjure thee, and all the oathes which I
And thou have sworne to seale joynt constancy,
Here I unsweare, and overswear them thus,
Thou shalt not love by wayes so dangerous.
Temper, ô faire Love, loves impetuous rage,
Be my true Mistris still, not my faign'd Page;
I'll goe, and, by thy kinde leave, leave behinde
Thee, onely worthy to nurse in my minde,
Thirst to come backe; ô if thou die before,
My soule from other lands to thee shall soare.
Thy (else Almighty) beautie cannot move
Rage from the Seas, nor thy love teach them love,
Nor tame wilde Boreas harshnesse; Thou hast read
How roughly hee in peeces shivered
Faire Orithea, whom he swore he lov'd.
Fall ill or good, 'tis madnesse to have prov'd
Dangers unurg'd; Feed on this flattery,
That absent Lovers one in th'other be.
Dissemble nothing, not a boy, nor change
Thy bodies habite, nor mindes; bee not strange
To thy selfe onely; All will spie in thy face
A blushing womanly discovering grace;
Richly cloath'd Apes, are call'd Apes, and as soone
Ecclips'd as bright we call the Moone the Moone.
Men of France, changeable Camelions,
Spittles of diseases, shops of fashions,
Loves fuellers, and the rightest company
Of Players, which upon the worlds stage be,
Will quickly know thee, and no lesse, alas!
Th'indifferent Italian, as we passe
His warme land, well content to thinke thee Page,
Will hunt thee with such lust, and hideous rage,
As *Lots* faire guests were vext. But none of these
Nor spungy hydroptique Dutch shall thee displease,
If thou stay here. O stay here, for, for thee
England is onely a worthy Gallerie,

To walke in expectation, till from thence
Our greatest King call thee to his presence.
When I am gone, dreame me some happinesse,
Nor let thy lookes our long hid love confesse,
Nor praise, nor dispraise me, nor blesse nor curse
Openly loves force, nor in bed fright thy Nurse
With midnights startings, crying out, oh, oh
Nurse, ô my love is slaine, I saw him goe
O'r the white Alpes alone; I saw him I,
Assail'd, fight, taken, stabb'd, bleed, fall, and die.
Augure me better chance, except dread *Jove*
Thinke it enough for me to'have had thy love.

AN EPITHALAMION, OR MARIAGE SONG

on the Lady Elizabeth, *and* Count Palatine
being married on St. Valentines *day*

I

HAILE Bishop Valentine, whose day this is,
    All the Aire is thy Diocis,
    And all the chirping Choristers
And other birds are thy Parishioners,
    Thou marryest every yeare
The Lirique Larke, and the grave whispering Dove,
The Sparrow that neglects his life for love,
The household Bird, with the red stomacher,
    Thou mak'st the black bird speed as soone,
As doth the Goldfinch, or the Halcyon;
The husband cocke lookes out, and straight is sped,
And meets his wife, which brings her feather-bed.
This day more cheerfully than ever shine,
This day, which might enflame thy self, Old Valentine.

II

Till now, Thou warmd'st with multiplying loves
    Two larkes, two sparrowes, or two Doves,
    All that is nothing unto this,
For thou this day couplest two Phœnixes;
    Thou mak'st a Taper see
What the sunne never saw, and what the Arke
(Which was of foules, and beasts, the cage, and park,)
Did not containe, one bed containes, through Thee,
    Two Phœnixes, whose joyned breasts
Are unto one another mutuall nests,

Where motion kindles such fires, as shall give
Yong Phœnixes, and yet the old shall live.
Whose love and courage never shall decline,
But make the whole year through, thy day, O Valentine.

III

Up then faire Phœnix Bride, frustrate the Sunne,
    Thy selfe from thine affection
      Takest warmth enough, and from thine eye
All lesser birds will take their Jollitie.
      Up, up, faire Bride, and call,
Thy starres, from out their severall boxes, take
Thy Rubies, Pearles, and Diamonds forth, and make
Thy selfe a constellation, of them All,
      And by their blazing, signifie,
That a Great Princess falls, but doth not die;
Bee thou a new starre, that to us portends
Ends of much wonder; And be Thou those ends.
Since thou dost this day in new glory shine,
May all men date Records, from this thy Valentine.

IIII

Come forth, come forth, and as one glorious flame
    Meeting Another, growes the same,
      So meet thy Fredericke, and so
To an unseparable union growe.
      Since separation
Falls not on such things as are infinite,
Nor things which are but one, can disunite,
You'are twice inseparable, great, and one;
      Goe then to where the Bishop staies,
To make you one, his way, which divers waies
Must be effected; and when all is past,

And that you'are one, by hearts and hands made fast,
You two have one way left, your selves to'entwine,
Besides this Bishops knot, or Bishop Valentine.

V

But oh, what ailes the Sunne, that here he staies,
    Longer to day, than other daies?
    Staies he new light from these to get?
And finding here such store, is loth to set?
    And why doe you two walke,
So slowly pac'd in this procession?
Is all your care but to be look'd upon,
And be to others spectacle, and talke?
    The feast, with gluttonous delaies,
Is eaten, and too long their meat they praise,
The masquers come too late, and'I thinke, will stay,
Like Fairies, till the Cock crow them away.
Alas, did not Antiquity assigne
A night, as well as day, to thee, O Valentine?

VI

They did, and night is come; and yet wee see
    Formalities retarding thee.
    What meane these Ladies, which (as though
They were to take a clock in peeces,) goe
    So nicely about the Bride;
A Bride, before a good night could be said,
Should vanish from her cloathes, into her bed,
As Soules from bodies steale, and are not spy'd.
    But now she is laid; What though shee bee?
Yet there are more delayes, For, where is he?
He comes, and passes through Spheare after Spheare,
First her sheetes, then her Armes, then any where.
Let not this day, then, but this night be thine,
Thy day was but the eve to this, O Valentine.

VII

Here lyes a shee Sunne, and a hee Moone here,
    She gives the best light to his Spheare,
    Or each is both, and all, and so
They unto one another nothing owe,
    And yet they doe, but are
So just and rich in that coyne which they pay,
That neither would, nor needs forbeare nor stay;
Neither desires to be spar'd, nor to spare,
    They quickly pay their debt, and then
Take no acquittances, but pay again;
They pay, they give, they lend, and so let fall
No such occasion to be liberall.
More truth, more courage in these two do shine,
Than all thy turtles have, and sparrows, Valentine.

VIII

And by this act of these two Phenixes
    Nature againe restored is,
    For since these two are two no more,
Ther's but one Phenix still, as was before.
    Rest now at last, and wee
As Satyres watch the Sunnes uprise, will stay
Waiting, when your eye opened, let out day,
Onely desir'd, because your face wee see;
    Others neare you shall whispering speake,
And wagers lay, at which side day will breake,
And win by'observing, then, whose hand it is
That opens first a curtaine, hers or his;
This will be tryed to morrow after nine,
Till which houre, wee thy day enlarge, O Valentine.

HOLY SONNETS

I

Thou hast made me, And shall thy worke decay?
Repaire me now, for now mine end doth haste,
I runne to death, and death meets me as fast,
And all my pleasures are like yesterday;
I dare not move my dimme eyes any way,
Despaire behind, and death before doth cast
Such terrour, and my feeble flesh doth waste
By sinne in it, which it t'wards hell doth weigh;
Onely thou art above, and when towards thee
By thy leave I can looke, I rise againe;
But our old subtle foe so tempteth me,
That not one houre my selfe I can sustaine;
Thy Grace may wing me to prevent his art,
And thou like Adamant draw mine iron heart.

II

As due by many titles I resign
My selfe to thee, O God, first I was made
By thee, and for thee, and when I was decay'd
Thy blood bought that, the which before was thine;
I am thy sonne, made with thy selfe to shine,
Thy servant, whose paines thou hast still repaid,
Thy sheepe, thine Image, and, till I betray'd
My selfe, a temple of thy Spirit divine;
Why doth the devill then usurpe on mee?
Why doth he steale, nay ravish that's thy right?

Except thou rise and for thine owne worke fight,
Oh I shall soone despaire, when I doe see
That thou lov'st mankind well, yet wilt'not chuse me,
And Satan hates mee, yet is loth to lose mee.

III

O MIGHT those sighes and teares returne againe
Into my breast and eyes, which I have spent,
That I might in this holy discontent
Mourne with some fruit, as I have mourn'd in vaine;
In mine Idolatry what showres of raine
Mine eyes did waste? what griefs my heart did rent?
That sufferance was my sinne; now I repent;
'Cause I did suffer I must suffer paine.
Th'hydroptique drunkard, and night-scouting thiefe,
The itchy Lecher, and selfe tickling proud
Have the remembrance of past joyes, for reliefe
Of comming ills. To (poore) me is allow'd
No ease; for, long, yet vehement griefe hath beene
Th'effect and cause, the punishment and sinne.

IV

OH my blacke Soule! now thou art summoned
By sicknesse, deaths herald, and champion;
Thou art like a pilgrim, which abroad hath done
Treason, and durst not turne to whence hee is fled,
Or like a thiefe, which till deaths doome be read,
Wisheth himselfe delivered from prison;
But damn'd and hal'd to execution,
Wisheth that still he might be imprisoned.
Yet grace, if thou repent, thou canst not lacke;
But who shall give thee that grace to beginne?
Oh make thy selfe with holy mourning blacke,

And red with blushing, as thou art with sinne;
Or wash thee in Christs blood, which hath this might
That being red, it dyes red soules to white.

V

I AM a little world made cunningly
Of Elements, and an Angelike spright,
But black sinne hath betraid to endlesse night
My worlds both parts, and (oh) both parts must die.
You which beyond that heaven which was most high
Have found new sphears, and of new lands can write,
Powre new seas in mine eyes, that so I might
Drowne my world with my weeping earnestly,
Or wash it if it must be drown'd no more:
But oh it must be burnt! alas the fire
Of lust and envie have burnt it heretofore,
And made it fouler; Let their flames retire,
And burne me ô Lord, with a fiery zeale
Of thee and thy house, which doth in eating heale

VI

THIS is my playes last scene, here heavens appoint
My pilgrimages last mile; and my race
Idly, yet quickly runne, hath this last pace,
My spans last inch, my minutes latest point,
And gluttonous death, will instantly unjoynt
My body, and soule, and I shall sleepe a space,
But my'ever-waking part shall see that face,
Whose feare already shakes my every joynt:
Then, as my soule, to'heaven her first seate, takes
     flight,
And earth-borne body, in the earth shall dwell,
So, fall my sinnes, that all may have their right,

To where they'are bred, and would presse me, to hell.
Impute me righteous, thus purg'd of evill,
For thus I leave the world, the flesh, the devill.

VII

At the round earths imagin'd corners, blow
Your trumpets, Angells, and arise, arise
From death, you numberlesse infinities
Of soules, and to your scattred bodies goe,
All whom the flood did, and fire shall o'erthrow,
All whom warre, dearth, age, agues, tyrannies,
Despaire, law, chance, hath slaine, and you whose
    eyes,
Shall behold God, and never tast deaths woe.
But let them sleepe, Lord, and mee mourne a space,
For, if above all these, my sinnes abound,
'Tis late to aske abundance of thy grace,
When wee are there; here on this lowly ground,
Teach mee how to repent; for that's as good
As if thou'hadst seal'd my pardon, with thy blood.

VIII

If faithfull soules be alike glorifi'd
As Angels, then my fathers soul doth see,
And adds this even to full felicitie,
That valiantly I hels wide mouth o'rstride:
But if our mindes to these soules be descry'd
By circumstances, and by signes that be
Apparent in us, not immediately,
How shall my mindes white truth by them be try'd?
They see idolatrous lovers weepe and mourne,
And vile blasphemous Conjurers to call
On Jesus name, and Pharisaicall

Dissemblers feigne devotion. Then turne
O pensive soule, to God, for he knowes best
Thy true griefe, for he put it in my breast.

IX

IF poysonous mineralls, and if that tree,
Whose fruit threw death on else immortall us,
If lecherous goats, if serpents envious
Cannot be damn'd; Alas; why should I bee?
Why should intent or reason, borne in mee,
Make sinnes, else equall, in mee more heinous?
And mercy being easie, and glorious
To God; in his sterne wrath, why threatens hee?
But who am I, that dare dispute with thee
O God? Oh! of thine onely worthy blood,
And my teares, make a heavenly Lethean flood,
And drowne in it my sinnes blacke memorie;
That thou remember them, some claime as debt,
I thinke it mercy, if thou wilt forget.

X

DEATH be not proud, though some have called thee
Mighty and dreadfull, for, thou art not soe,
For, those, whom thou think'st, thou dost overthrow,
Die not, poore death, nor yet canst thou kill mee.
From rest and sleepe, which but thy pictures bee,
Much pleasure, then from thee, much more must flow
And soonest our best men with thee doe goe,
Rest of their bones, and soules deliverie.
Thou art slave to Fate, Chance, kings, and desperate
  men,
And dost with poyson, warre, and sicknesse dwell,
And poppie, or charmes can make us sleepe as well,

And better than thy stroake; why swell'st thou then?
One short sleepe past, wee wake eternally,
And death shall be no more; death, thou shalt die.

XI

Spit in my face you Jewes, and pierce my side,
Buffet, and scoffe, scourge, and crucifie mee,
For I have sinn'd, and sinn'd, and onely hee,
Who could do no iniquitie, hath dyed:
But by my death can not be satisfied
My sinnes, which passe the Jewes impiety:
They kill'd once an inglorious man, but I
Crucifie him daily, being now glorified.
Oh let mee then, his strange love still admire:
Kings pardon, but he bore our punishment.
And *Jacob* came cloth'd in vile harsh attire
But to supplant, and with gainfull intent:
God cloth'd himselfe in vile mans flesh, that so
Hee might be weake enough to suffer woe.

XII

Why are wee by all creatures waited on?
Why doe the prodigall elements supply
Life and food to mee, being more pure than I,
Simple, and further from corruption?
Why brook'st thou, ignorant horse, subjection?
Why dost thou bull, and bore so seelily
Dissemble weaknesse, and by'one mans stroke die,
Whose whole kinde, you might swallow and feed upon?
Weaker I am, woe is mee, and worse than you,
You have not sinn'd, nor need be timorous.
But wonder at a greater wonder, for to us
Created nature doth these things subdue.

But their Creator, whom sin, nor nature tyed,
For us, his Creatures, and his foes, hath dyed.

XIII

WHAT if this present were the worlds last night?
Marke in my heart, O Soule, where thou dost dwell,
The picture of Christ crucified, and tell
Whether that countenance can thee affright,
Teares in his eyes quench the amazing light,
Blood fills his frownes, which from his pierc'd head fell.
And can that tongue adjudge thee unto hell,
Which pray'd forgivenesse for his foes fierce spight?
No, no; but as in my idolatrie
I said to all my profane mistresses,
Beauty, of pitty, foulnesse onely is
A signe of rigour: so I say to thee,
To wicked spirits are horrid shapes assign'd,
This beauteous forme assures a pitious minde.

XIV

BATTER my heart, three person'd God; for, you
As yet but knocke, breathe, shine, and seeke to mend;
That I may rise, and stand, o'erthrow mee,'and bend
Your force, to breake, blowe, burn and make me new
I, like an usurpt towne, to'another due,
Labour to'admit you, but Oh, to no end,
Reason your viceroy in mee, mee should defend,
But is captiv'd, and proves weake or untrue.
Yet dearely'I love you,'and would be loved faine,
But am betroth'd unto your enemie:
Divorce mee,'untie, or breake that knot againe,
Take mee to you, imprison mee, for I
Except you'enthrall mee, never shall be free,
Nor ever chast, except you ravish mee.

XV

WILT thou love God, as he thee? then digest,
My Soule, this wholsome meditation,
How God the Spirit, by Angels waited on
In heaven, doth make his Temple in thy brest.
The Father having begot a Sonne most blest,
And still begetting, (for he ne'r begonne)
Hath deign'd to chuse thee by adoption,
Coheire to'his glory,'and Sabbaths endlesse rest;
And as a robb'd man, which by search doth finde
His stolne stuffe sold, must lose or buy'it againe:
The Sonne of glory came downe, and was slaine,
Us whom he'had made, and Satan stolne, to unbinde.
'Twas much, that man was made like God before,
But, that God should be made like man, much more.

XVI

FATHER, part of his double interest
Unto thy kingdome, thy Sonne gives to mee,
His joynture in the knottie Trinitie
Hee keepes, and gives to me his deaths conquest.
This Lambe, whose death, with life the world hath
    blest,
Was from the worlds beginning slaine, and he
Hath made two Wills, which with the Legacie
Of his and thy kingdome, doe thy Sonnes invest.
Yet such are thy laws, that men argue yet
Whether a man those statutes can fulfill;
None doth; but all-healing grace and spirit
Revive againe what law and letter kill.
Thy lawes abridgement, and thy last command
Is all but love; Oh let this last Will stand!

XVII

SINCE she whom I lov'd hath payd her last debt
To Nature, and to hers, and my good is dead,
And her Soule early into heaven ravished,
Wholly on heavenly things my mind is sett.
Here the admyring her my mind did whett
To seeke thee God; so streames do shew their head;
But though I have found thee, and thou my thirst hast
      fed,
A holy thirsty dropsy melts mee yett.
But why should I begg more Love, when as thou
Dost wooe my soule for hers; offring all thine:
And dost not only feare least I allow
My Love to Saints and Angels things divine,
But in thy tender jealosy dost doubt
Least the World, Fleshe, yea Devill putt thee out.

XVIII

SHOW me deare Christ, thy Spouse, so bright and clear.
What! is it She, which on the other shore
Goes richly painted? or which rob'd and tore
Laments and mournes in Germany and here?
Sleepes she a thousand, then peepes up one yeare?
Is she selfe truth and errs? now new, now outwore?
Doth she, and did she, and shall she evermore
On one, on seaven, or on no hill appeare?
Dwells she with us, or like adventuring knights
First travaile we to seeke and then make Love?
Betray kind husband thy spouse to our sights,
And let myne amorous soule court thy mild Dove,
Who is most trew, and pleasing to thee, then
When she'is embrac'd and open to most men.

XIX

Oh, to vex me, contraryes meet in one:
Inconstancy unnaturally hath begott
A constant habit; that when I would not
I change in vowes, and in devotione.
As humorous is my contritione
As my prophane Love, and as soone forgott:
As ridlingly distemper'd, cold and hott,
As praying, as mute; as infinite, as none.
I durst not view heaven yesterday; and to day
In prayers, and flattering speaches I court God:
To morrow I quake with true feare of his rod.
So my devout fitts come and go away
Like a fantastique Ague: save that here
Those are my best dayes, when I shake with feare

GOODFRIDAY, 1613. RIDING WESTWARD

Let mans Soule be a Spheare, and then, in this,
The intelligence that moves, devotion is,
And as the other Spheares, by being growne
Subject to forraigne motions, lose their owne,
And being by others hurried every day,
Scarce in a yeare their naturall forme obey:
Pleasure or businesse, so, our Soules admit
For their first mover, and are whirld by it.
Hence is't, that I am carryed towards the West
This day, when my Soules forme bends toward the East.
There I should see a Sunne, by rising set,
And by that setting endlesse day beget;
But that Christ on this Crosse, did rise and fall,
Sinne had eternally benighted all.

Yet dare I'almost be glad, I do not see
That spectacle of too much weight for mee.
Who sees Gods face, that is selfe life, must dye;
What a death were it then to see God dye?
It made his owne Lieutenant Nature shrinke,
It made his footstoole crack, and the Sunne winke.
Could I behold those hands which span the Poles,
And tune all spheares at once, peirc'd with those holes?
Could I behold that endlesse height which is
Zenith to us, and our Antipodes,
Humbled below us? or that blood which is
The seat of all our Soules, if not of his,
Made durt of dust, or that flesh which was worne
By God, for his apparell, rag'd, and torne?
If on these things I durst not looke, durst I
Upon his miserable mother cast mine eye,
Who was Gods partner here, and furnish'd thus
Halfe of that Sacrifice, which ransom'd us?
Though these things, as I ride, be from mine eye,
They'are present yet unto my memory,
For that looks towards them; and thou look'st towards
      mee,
O Saviour, as thou hang'st upon the tree;
I turne my backe to thee, but to receive
Corrections, till thy mercies bid thee leave.
O thinke mee worth thine anger, punish mee,
Burne off my rusts, and my deformity,
Restore thine Image, so much, by thy grace,
That thou may'st know mee, and I'll turne my face.

A HYMNE TO GOD THE FATHER

I

Wɪʟᴛ thou forgive that sinne where I begunne,
  Which is my sin, though it were done before?
Wilt thou forgive those sinnes, through which I runne,
  And do run still: though still I do deplore?
    When thou hast done, thou hast not done,
      For, I have more.

II

Wilt thou forgive that sinne by which I'have wonne
  Others to sinne? and, made my sinne their doore?
Wilt thou forgive that sinne which I did shunne
  A yeare, or two: but wallowed in, a score?
    When thou hast done, thou hast not done,
      For I have more.

III

I have a sinne of feare, that when I have spunne
  My last thred, I shall perish on the shore;
Sweare by thy selfe, that at my death thy sonne
  Shall shine as he shines now, and heretofore;
    And, having done that, Thou haste done,
      I feare no more.

NOTES AND COMMENTARY

SONGS AND SONETS

1. THE GOOD-MORROW
Our love is unique. All other pleasures are mere
fancy, and all previous experience as unreal as a dream.
We are, each to each, a complete world, like the two
hemispheres, but without change or decline. Our love
cannot change, because it is equal on both sides.

*v.*1. *the seaven sleepers* of Ephesus slept in a cave for
187 years.

1. SONG
A cynical reflection on the inconstancy of fair women.
After suggesting a number of impossibilities, he asks the
hearer to find him a woman both "true and fair". "Even if
you do," he concludes, "it would be useless, because by
the time I reached her, she would have betrayed two or
three other men."

*v.*1. *mandrake roote:* the mandrake was a plant supposed
to have some human functions, but not that of child-
bearing.

2. THE UNDERTAKING
A poem on Platonic love. He claims to have found a
virtuous woman, whom he loves for her virtue and not
her sex. This is a braver undertaking than anything
done by the nine worthies (men of high moral character);
it would be still braver to keep quiet about it; for since
others might not find such a woman, they would merely
return to their former fleshly love (just as it would be
foolish to impart the skill of cutting magical stones when
no such stone could be found to work on). Nevertheless,

love of the soul makes loathsome the love of the body; and if anyone else achieves such love and declares it to the woman but hides it from worldly men, who would either disbelieve or scorn him, then he too has done a brave thing.

3. THE SUNNE RISING

He derisively tells the rising sun to leave him alone with his mistress, and attend to other matters. "Why do you imagine your beams all-powerful, when I could blot them out by closing my eyes, though I would not do so, for I would not lose sight of her even for an instant. When you have next been round the earth, you will find that both the East Indies (famous for spices) and the West Indies (famous for gold) are not where they were before, but here with me; while all the kings of the earth are here in bed—for she is the world and I am its ruler. We are the only true reality. You are old and seek comfort; your duty is to warm the world; it is done in warming us, since we *are* the whole world."

4. THE INDIFFERENT

I can love any woman as long as she is inconstant. Are women in search of new vices? Are they afraid that perhaps men are constant? Let them not fear this— men are as untrue as they. I desire as many mistresses as a woman has lovers. Venus, Goddess of Love, insists on inconstancy among her followers; the few women who disobey her by being true shall be punished by having false lovers.

5. LOVES USURY

A cynical comment on fashionable love-making, in the form of an offer to the god of love that, for each hour of his youth in which he is spared from true love he will devote twenty in his middle age. Provided he may behave like any fashionable and insincere man about town while he is young, he will put up with the afflictions of being truly in love when he is older—even with a woman who is in love with him.

6. THE CANONIZATION

He tells others to mind their own business and let him love in peace. Various ways in which Donne's fashionable friends might occupy themselves are suggested, such as travelling or trying to obtain a "place" (i.e., a position of importance) by cultivating a lord or a bishop, attending upon the king or amassing money (i.e., coins with the king's face stamped on them). The affairs of the world are in no way affected by my love. Whatever we are, even though you think us as insignificant as flies, my mistress and I are made such by love. In us two fierceness and gentleness are combined. We represent the perfect union of male and female. If we cannot live by love alone, we can die by it and form the subject if not of history, at least of poetry. Our love songs will be the hymns of a new religion, of which we will be the saints. We shall be worshipped as the patterns of perfect love.

v.2. *plaguie Bill:* a weekly list of deaths from the plague.

v.3. *Phœnix ridle:* The mystery of the fabulous bird which burnt itself to death every 500 years, rising anew from its own ashes. Donne means that he and his mistress were continually revived after being consumed in the fire of passion.

v.4. *sonnets pretty roomes:* the stanzas of a love song. (Italian, *stanza* .. room.)

8. THE TRIPLE FOOL

He is a fool for falling in love: but how could even a wise man help this? He is a fool for writing love poems: but he hoped this might ease his pain. He is once more a fool when both love and pain are increased by hearing his poems set to music and sung.

8. LOVERS INFINITENESSE

An elaborate intellectual argument (suggested by Donne's studies in the law) based on the paradox that love continues to grow even after it has seemed whole and complete. I have no further means to make you love me more. If when our love was first declared, you withheld some of your love, then some of it must be owing to other men. Other men may outbid me for possession of your love. Even if I had all your love originally, I fear you may have conceived new love which does not belong to me. And yet it does, for you gave me your heart, including everything that might grow in it. But if I have all your love, then I may never have more; and my love, which daily grows more, demands more in return. We cannot keep giving each other our hearts: the only solution is to join them; then we shall have all of each other.

10. SONG

Saintsbury thinks that this beautiful valediction, like *A Valediction: forbidding Mourning* (p. 33), and *Elegy XVI* (p. 70), was written on leaving for the Continent in 1611. According to Walton, his wife 'professed an unwillingness to allow him any absence from her; saying, "Her divining soul boded her some ill in his absence"; and therefore desired him not to leave her'.

A number of different but connected ideas are here expressed.

v.1. I do not leave you because I want to; but death will part us in the end, and absence is a sort of rehearsal of death.

v.2. The sun returns daily; my journey will be as swift and my return even more certain.

v.3. We only add to our unhappiness by making it seem longer than it really is.

v.4. By sighing and weeping you only waste yourself away.

If you love me as much as you say, you could not sigh and weep, because by so doing you waste away yourself, which is the better part of me.

v.5. Do not imagine any misfortune will befall me; instead, think of our separation merely as a sleep. Those who truly love are never parted.

11. A FEAVER

Donne is evidently worried about his mistress' fever, and incapable of writing his best poetry. The argument is forced and intellectual—what we might call 'wishful thinking'. But there is true feeling, as he tries to reason away his fear.

Do not die of this fever, for I shall not be able to praise you truly. You will not die, for if you do, the whole world will dissolve. Or if you leave the world, it will be no more than your corpse, the fairest woman your ghost and the worthiest men only worms.

Did no Jesuitical theologian, arguing about the source of the fire in which the world would finally be destroyed, have the sense to guess that your fever might be it? Yet you cannot suffer this wasting torment for long, for a long-burning fire requires much matter for fuel.

These feverish fits are like mere shooting stars and do not burn away much of you; your beauty—indeed, every part of you—is incorruptible heavenly substance. Yet although this fever cannot persist long, in seizing hold of you it did as I would do; for I would rather possess you for an hour than anything else for ever.

v.4–5. Notice the change of pronoun here from *thou* to *she*.

v.5. For *much* the original text gives *such*, but I cannot make sense of this.

12. AIRE AND ANGELS

The highly intellectualised nature of the argument is here so refined that it eludes comprehension. The following attempt to simplify it sacrifices a great deal of its subtlety.

Just as angels appear in the sound of a voice or in a flame, so you appeared to me before I knew you; and whenever I was near you, I was aware of your presence. My love, the child of my soul, could not be active unless it took bodily form; my love has fixed itself in your features. But all your beauty proved too much for my love to work on, for love cannot live either in nothing or in an excess of objects; since my love cannot reside in your features, it must reside in your love, just as an angel wears a face and wings of air. Air is a little more pure and insubstantial than angels; just so much difference exists between woman's love and man's.

13. BREAKE OF DAY

An appeal by a woman to her lover to stay with her. What has love, she says, to do with the time of day? The worst that can be said against her is that she wants to stay with the man who has her heart and honour. Let him not tell her he has work to do—a busy man has no right to make love.

14. THE ANNIVERSARIE

It is a year since we first fell in love. Everything except our love is a year nearer to final destruction. When we die, our bodies will be separated; but our souls, in which our love alone lives, will leave our bodies. We shall then enjoy perfect happiness—but no more than anyone else. It is here on earth, while we are still alive, that our true greatness appears. We two are each other's kings: and no other king ever had such subjects, nor was so safe from treason. Let us have no fears, real or imaginary, but live to enjoy a long and happy life.

v.2. *inmates:* lodgers, visitors.

15. A VALEDICTION: OF MY NAME, IN THE WINDOW

Donne here reveals an interesting state of mind. Does he really mistrust the woman he is leaving, or is it (as he says in the last verse) misery at their approaching separation that breeds mistrust? Before leaving her he has scratched his name with a diamond in a pane of her window. The glass, he says, has now acquired my strength, and your looking at it will give it the value of diamonds. Glass is as transparent (honest) as I; what is more, it can reflect your beauty. But since, by love's magic, I am you, the glass can show me to you when I am gone. Just as no storm can wash away even a dot or stroke of my name, so nothing can make me false; you should find it still easier to be true, because you have this example continuously before you. But if this argument is too far-fetched, then treat my name as a reminder of lovers' mortality: regard this scratched signature as my skeleton. Then since my soul is with you, its paradise, my flesh will return to join my bones.

Until I come back reconstruct my body so, in imagination. Stars in the ascendant influence our characters: when this name was engraved, love and grief were in the ascendant; therefore you should be more loving and more sad during my absence, and mourn for me daily.

When you open the window to look at some new suitor, imagine that you are offending my living spirit, and when your maid has been bribed to bring you my rival's letter and has calmed your annoyance, so that you begin to look kindly on him, then may my name intervene and cover his signature; and if you should go so far as actually to answer his letter, may your mind be moved to address your letter to me and not my rival. Your mistake will cause you to do right, and you will write to me unawares. But it is not my name scratched on glass which will keep us faithful in love. Our approaching separation makes me ramble in my talk: separation is death, and the tongues of dying men often wander.

v.1. *of either rock:* from the west (South America) or
the east (India).

v.6. *such characters:* there is a play on the two meanings
of the word—written letters and human character.

17. TWICKNAM GARDEN

This poem, with its irregular first line, expresses
extreme agitation, bitterness and distress. But the
occasion of it is, perhaps deliberately, kept secret.
Donne does not tell us what the "disgrace" is (*v*.2) nor
in what way the woman "kills him by her truth" (*v*.3).
About one thing only there is no doubt—the passionate
intensity of his feelings.

In these gardens in spring I would find comfort for
any woe but that the poisonous spider, love, turns all to
bitterness and that I bring with me the serpent jealousy.
Winter would be more in key with my mood. In order
not to feel my disgrace and yet be still in love, I wish I
might be either a mandrake root (half-human plant) or
a stone fountain. Let lovers test the truth of their
mistresses' protestations by comparing their tears with
mine: for you cannot judge of a woman's love by her
looks nor of her thoughts by her tears. She whose truth
kills me is the only one of her sex who is true.

18. A VALEDICTION: OF THE BOOKE

When we are separated, you can be as glorious as any
of the women who helped poets in times past (Sybilla,
authoress of prophetic books; Corinna, rival of the Greek
poet Pindar; Polla Argentaria, wife of the Latin poet
Lucan, or the Egyptian poetess Phantasia, whose works
were said to have inspired Homer). Compile from our
letters the history of our love for the example of future
lovers; such a book would be free from the attack of any
heretic (*schismatique*).

Our book, permanent as the world itself and written

in the language of poetry—we being only the agents for love's official priests—will preserve love's learning against any further ravages of Vandals and Goths. It will be a new universe for the study of astrology; it will provide a new music of the spheres and new songs for the angels.

Here students of love may find all they look for, whether abstract spiritual love, or love based on physical beauty. Lawyers will find out the true legal position of men in relation to their mistresses; they will find also how women claim more than what is due to them, giving nothing in return, and in forsaking their lovers giving honour or conscience as the reason.

In our book politicians—or such of them as can read—will find justification for their activities: for in politics, as in love, provided things go well, no one troubles to enquire into principle.

Meanwhile, I will consider you from afar, for that is the best way to judge how long our love will last. Love's strength is best measured in times of happiness; its extent in times of misery and separation.

*v.*1. *Esloygne:* banish (French, *éloigner*).

20. LOVES GROWTH

Love is not so pure and abstract as poets would have us believe who have no mistress but the Muse, their imaginary source of inspiration. I find my love has grown since the winter, and that it endures change, like the seasons. Love is sometimes contemplative or dormant, as in winter; sometimes active and growing, as in spring.

However, by its growth love becomes not greater, but brighter, just as the planets are revealed, not increased, by the sun's light. In spring love becomes active. Each spring adds to love what no winter removes, as rulers impose new taxes in war but do not take them off in times of peace.

21. LOVES EXCHANGE

A bitter denunciation of love, which he had formerly defied; he now finds himself humiliated by the agony of unrequited love.

At court some men give their souls for writing verse, hunting or gambling; I have given my soul to the devil Love and got nothing in exchange. I do not now ask permission to pretend that my lover's tears, sighs and vows are false. They are an inevitable consequence of being in love: I could not deny them unless I denied being in love. I beg only to be made blind, so that I may not know the true shame of loving without reward.

Yet Love is right to give nothing, since I would not at first trust him—just as small towns which are besieged cannot make conditions with the enemy when once they have defied him. That is my situation: I was at first sceptical about love, but later I defied him and now find him to be an all-powerful conqueror. Thus enraged against me, Love takes his revenge. I beg him not to torture me but kill me outright. If I am to be dissected for the instruction of future lovers, my body had better not be disfigured on the rack.

23. THE DREAME

Donne tells his mistress that she woke him in the midst of a vivid and passionate dream of her. "Let us," he says, "continue the dream in reality." When she first woke him by her radiance, he thought her an angel. Then realising that she read his thoughts, he knew that she could be no other than herself. He hoped she came to him as a lover, her love unmixed with any sense of fear or shame.

24. A VALEDICTION: OF WEEPING

Donne is about to go overseas, and this is an expression of the intense misery which the parting causes. The poem may be over-intellectual and the imagery hyperbolical, but this kind of expression is characteristic of Donne's continual attempts to put into words a feeling which overflows expression.

Let me weep where my tears can reflect your face and so acquire value, like minted coins. Our separation reduces us both to nothing. These tears, reflecting your image, are like worlds; your tears, falling like rain from heaven, mix with mine and overflow the world. Do not drown me, as the sea may soon do, with the excess of your grief; let not our sighs teach the wind to blow. Let us not sigh away one another's life.

25. LOVES ALCHYMIE

Some lovers claim to have discovered the very centre, the innermost core, of love. I, though I should make love till I am old, will never make such a boast. It is mere imposture. Just as those learned in chemistry, if they should, while seeking the unattainable elixir, come across some pleasant by-product, will boast of their discoveries—so lovers, dreaming of deep and lasting felicity, get only a brief pleasure.

Should we, then, exchange for such an empty, short-lived thing as love all our worldly benefits? Cannot my servant be as happy as I if he is prepared to put up with the brief farce of marriage? The man who says that he marries not a woman's body but her angelic mind, would be as ready to swear that the crude music of a wedding ceremony is the music of the spheres. Do not hope for minds in women; even the sweetest and most intelligent, once you possess them, you find to be mere dead flesh.

v.1. Elixar: the ultimate aim of the alchemist's researches; a liquid either for turning base metals into gold or for prolonging life.

25. THE FLEA

Ingenious as it is, this is as cynical and unpleasant a poem as any Donne wrote. It is, no doubt, deliberately shocking. Yet to ignore such manifestations of his nature and wit would be as mistaken as to ignore his idealistic side.

Why do you deny me the mixture of our two bloods, which takes place within this flea when he goes from me to you? Do not kill it, for in doing so you kill both yourself and me as well.

Now that you have killed it, you see that it makes no difference to us after all. As little of your life is lost by its death, just so little honour you lose by yielding to me.

26.   THE CURSE

A comprehensive curse on anyone who thinks he knows who Donne's mistress is. No doubt he is working off a fit of malicious anger against a meddling acquaintance or rival. The most outrageous evils are wished upon the unfortunate meddler. The concluding savage joke about women is characteristic. If sheer ill-temper is ever magnificent, it is so in this poem.

27.   THE MESSAGE

A bitter love-song, contrasting violently with the courtly fashion of his day.

He asks his false mistress to return his eyes and heart, which in love he had given her. "No, keep them," he says, "for they will have learnt falseness and cruelty from you. Yet return them to me, false and cruel as they are, because with them I shall be able to exult over you when some man treats you as you have treated me."

28.   A NOCTURNALL UPON S. LUCIES DAY

This poem expresses the death of the soul felt at the loss of someone he loved. One of the most intense and passionate Donne ever wrote.

On this the shortest day of the year (a day in mid-December) all life seems to have shrunk into the earth; and I feel even more dead than anything else. Where love springs up afresh after the deadness of winter, let lovers consider me. I died of love, but am reborn from absence, death and darkness, which are the very quintessence of nothingness. Others draw their life from whatever is good; my being is as it were distilled by love out of every negation of life—tears, neglect of each other, or the agony of separation. Her death makes me the very essence of nothingness. Human beings and animals, even plants and stones, have some properties; even a shadow is caused by light and form, but I am none of those things; the sun of my life will not return. At this time the sun is in the sign of the Goat (symbol of lust); when he returns, may other lovers enjoy their love. Let me prepare to go to my dead mistress.

30. WITCHCRAFT BY A PICTURE

A curious and elaborate thought on the subject of parting. He sees his reflection both in her eye and in a tear, and imagines what power she would have over him had she the witchcraft to kill by means of a picture. (This refers to a belief common on Donne's time.) He ends by saying that he leaves his image in her heart, where it is free from all malice.

30. THE BAITE

It was fashionable among poets of Donne's time to write imitations of Marlowe's *Come, live with me and be my love*. This is Donne's attempt, characteristic in its elaborate artificiality of thought, but deliberately smoother and more melodious than usual in its versification.

31. THE APPARITION

A piece of savage joking addressed to a woman who refuses his advances.

Killed by her scorn, he says, his ghost will appear

to her when she is in the arms of another. When her candle goes out, she will appeal to her lover for help; fatigued by love, he will ignore her, and she will be left to lie in terror. What the ghost will say, Donne keeps secret, so as to spare her no terror. Since he no longer loves her, he would rather that she should painfully repent her treatment of him than that, by knowing what he threatens, she should preserve herself unharmed.

32. THE BROKEN HEART

No man can be in love for so long as an hour, since love is too violent to last so long. Love takes entire possession of our hearts, swallowing us whole, as a pike swallows little fish. What has happened to my heart since I first saw you? You shattered it to pieces; the fragments fill my breast. Just as a broken mirror gives many reflections, so the fragments of my heart feel affection, desire and adoration, but never love again.

33. A VALEDICTION: FORBIDDING MOURNING

Said to have been given to his wife on leaving for the continent in 1611 (see note on *Song*, p. 10).

Let our parting be silent and imperceptible, like the dying breath of a good man; let not violent sorrow show the world how much we love. Mere earthquakes cause fear and alarm: when the whole of creation moves, the movement is greater but causes no shock. The love of ordinary lovers is only of the senses, and is destroyed if absence separates their bodies. But our love is of so pure an essence, being assured of existence in each other's minds, that it is less disturbed by the separation of our bodies. Our two souls are one: my parting does not divide, but rather expands, them, like gold beaten out thin. We are like the two legs of a pair of compasses, yours the fixed one in the centre. The further my soul goes from yours, the more yours leans towards mine; and as mine comes home, so yours revives. Your soul is the centre of my being, and keeps mine constant as it circles around you.

34. THE EXTASIE

The extraordinary subtlety and refinement of this argument on physical and spiritual love defies analysis and makes close paraphrase impossible. It appears to be Donne at his most characteristic: in it he achieves for once the perfect reconciliation of the physical and the spiritual which he was seeking in so much of his poetic thought.

· We lay together on a bank with our hands joined, gazing into one another's eyes. There was as yet no closer union. Our souls, leaving our bodies, parleyed with one another like opposing armies. If anyone with a mind so refined by love that he could understand the language of souls happened to be listening, he would take on a purer essence from our souls' conversation. This ecstacy (that is, the temporary separation of soul from body) taught us what we did not know before— that it was not sex which moved us to love one another. Two souls are united by love: transplant a violet and you improve the strain. The single soul which grows out of the union of two is finer than either singly. We are now composed only of the unchangeable material of souls. But why do we deny our bodies, which after all belong to us? They are the sphere in which we, the soul, move. Our physical senses brought us first together; our bodies, of which our senses are a part, are not mere dross to be cast side, but a sort of dilution of the soul. Just as the influence of the stars affect men only through the air, so souls are united only through the agency of the body. As our blood strives to produce the vital energies without which we cannot function as men, so the souls of lovers must express themselves through physical communication; otherwise love cannot express itself, and the future remains like a prince in prison. Let our souls, then, return to our bodies, so that in our physical union ordinary men may see the mystery of love revealed (like religious mystery revealed in the Bible). And if our eavesdropping lover sees our souls return to our bodies, he will find us little changed.

36. LOVES DEITIE

Before love was made a god, no lover would have stooped to love one who did not love him. But now the God of Love has ordained that I shall love unloved. This cannot have been Love's original plan: true love is equal on both sides. Now, however, Love has become a tyrant, all-powerful as Jove himself, and under his sway I behave like one infatuated. If only men could rebel and overturn Love's tyranny, I would not suffer this unrequited love. But I am not only a rebel against Love, I am also an unbeliever; it would be worse not to be in love with her, or else to have her love. For she loves another, and it is better that she should hate me than that she should be false.

37. THE FUNERALL

Donne imagines himself dying of love, with a strand of his mistress' hair bound round his arm. He orders that it should be buried with him, since it symbolises his soul and will keep his body from dissolution when his soul has left it, for if his soul (the *sinewie thread* from his own brain) can keep his body united, how much better can the hair from his mistress' head do it. Perhaps, however, she gave it to him to signify his enslavement to her, like the manacles on a condemned prisoner. Whatever its meaning, it must be buried with him, for otherwise lovers might begin to worship it as a relic. Since he was humble enough to take it as a symbol of his soul, so he is proud enough to bury a part of her who is content to let him die.

38. THE BLOSSOME

The significance of the flower in the first verse does not seem to me as clear as the rest of the poem, whose sense could well begin at verse 2. Possibly the flower signifies simply Love; if so, Donne seems to change his mind and abandon the image after verse 1. But this is not the only poem in the course of which his line of thought takes new directions.

The flower whose birth and growth I have watched will fall and die to-morrow. My heart, which like a bird has been trying to build a nest in the unyielding tree of her love, must make a journey to-morrow. My heart protests that it need not take this journey with my body, but would prefer to stay behind with her. Let my heart stay behind, then, but it will be useless; for, having no heart herself, she will not recognise my heart when my body is absent. Let my heart rejoin me in London three weeks hence, where it will find me fatter and more contented; let my heart be so too, for I will give it to another woman—one who will be as pleased to have my body as my mind.

39. THE RELIQUE

It was the custom in Donne's time to make new graves on the site of old ones, which were often quite shallow. (See the gravedigging scene in *Hamlet*.) Compare *The Funerall*, p. 37.

When my grave is broken open for another body, will not he who discovers my skeleton with the bracelet of bright hair around my arm leave my bones in peace, realising that this symbolises two souls perfectly united which shall meet on the day of judgement? If this should happen when idolatrous religion is practised, you and I will be worshipped as saints. If miracles are looked for, then let me tell what miracles we performed: first, we were true and faithful lovers; secondly, we were not conscious of the difference of sex between us; thirdly, we

exchanged only the formal kisses customary on visiting
for meals; fourthly, we never broke the bond of marriage.
(The sense of these lines is doubtful.) These miracles we
performed, but you yourself were a greater miracle than
all.

41. THE DAMPE

When your disdain has killed me, and doctors cut me
up to find the cause, your picture in my heart will
strike them all down with an ague of love; the murder
you have committed on me will then be promoted
(*preferred*) to the status of a massacre. This will be a
poor victory: if you want to conquer me gloriously, then
first slay your own disdain and honour, and destroy the
records of your former triumphs; for I could call in on
my side such allies as constancy and secrecy, but I
neither expect these from you nor make a profession
of them myself. Kill me simply as a woman, and I will
die simply as a man. With nothing on your side but
womanhood, you will still have sufficient advantage
over me.

41. A JEAT RING SENT

My heart is as black and her faith as brittle as the jet
ring she sent me. What can it signify but that my faith
is endless and hers brittle? Why should anything less
durable than the pure gold of a wedding ring symbolise
our love—unless she has bidden this ring to speak for
her and say "I am worthless; my love is mere fashion;
throw me away"? Nevertheless, I will keep the ring;
it will be safer in my hands than in the hands of her who
would break it as easily as she broke her faith.

42. THE PROHIBITION

Do not love me too much: not that I shall make you
suffer what I suffered for you before. But the excess of
joy which your falling in love with me would cause might

kill me and so frustrate your love. Yet do not hate me: this would be to triumph too much in your victory over me. Not that I would take the law into my hands and retaliate by hating you; no, but you could lose the title of conqueror if I were to die from your hate. Both love and hate me, so that neither extreme may have its full effect (that of killing me). Let extreme love and hate cancel one another out. Alive, I shall be like a stage on which your victory is daily enacted, and not a conqueror's triumph in which I would perish once for all. In order that you should not destroy your love, your hate, and me as well, love and hate me at the same time, and so preserve my life.

42. THE EXPIRATION

We must part; let us not wait till someone comes to part us; we asked no one's leave to love, nor need we be beholden to anyone for the word of parting. Go, then; and if you still have life, kill me by telling me to go. If you are dead already, may my own word kill me, your murderer—unless I am already doubly dead by parting from you and telling you to go.

43. THE COMPUTATION

For the first twenty years since we parted yesterday I could not believe you had gone; for the next forty I lived on the thought of your past kindness; for the next forty I lived on the hope that you wanted to prolong this kindness; tears and sighs accounted for another 300; 1,000 passed in thoughtless inaction—or else I spent them in a single thought of you; for another 1,000 I forgot what that thought was. But do not imagine I have spent a long life since yesterday. I am dead, and so immortal. Shall I ever die, being a ghost?

44. THE PARADOX

This poem shows the ingenuity of Donne's intellectual play on ideas. He here elaborates an obscure argument

based on one of the commonplaces of his thought—
namely, that extreme love kills the lover. The following
is not a very satisfactory attempt at paraphrase.

Every lover thinks he is the only perfect lover. I
cannot say I was in love formerly (because love is so
strong that it kills the lover). Love kills the young
with heat, death kills the old with cold. We can only
die once; whoever says he has died twice is a liar: any
appearance of life in a man after he has been in love is
only an illusion—such life is like the light after sunset or
the warmth that remains after substances have been
heated. I am one who died of love, and am no more than
my own grave and epitaph.

44. FAREWELL TO LOVE

In my ignorance I once thought there was some
divinity in love and like an unconvinced atheist I
honoured it. So we covet unknown things and fashion
them according to our desires. As children admire a
gingerbread king brought home from the fair, so lovers
desire the false image of divinity in love; but once they
begin to enjoy it, it decays. That which first charmed
them entirely now pleases only the sexual appetite, and
leaves the mind dull and depressed. Why cannot
humans, like cocks and lions, be joyful after the act of
love? The curse of mortality (*being short*) sharpens the
desire to produce children and so achieve immortality.
(According to Grierson, the word *eagers* is not an adjective
but an obsolete verb). But the act of love shortens life
(so it was believed in Donne's time)—perhaps, therefore,
nature in her wisdom causes us this depression after love.
Since I can find no divinity in love, I will no longer
pursue what has only harmed me; I will therefore admire
beautiful women from a safe distance. If this fails, it is
because I have set about curing myself in the wrong way.

46. A LECTURE UPON THE SHADOW

Just as we tread on our shadows now that it is noon, so we seem to have overcome the cares and troubles which grew from our love in its infancy. Love which is still concerned with secrecy has not reached its height. But in its maturity our love may produce new cares to trouble ourselves. If our love begins to decline, we shall begin to be secretive towards each other. How short is love's noon when once it begins to decline. As soon as it is past its zenith, night falls swiftly upon it.

47. SONNET. THE TOKEN

He asks his mistress to give him for his comfort none of the usual presents (ribbon, ring, bracelet, picture or verses), but only her assurance that she believes him in love with her.

EPIGRAMS

48. A BURNT SHIP

This reminds us that England was at war with Spain during Donne's youth, and that he sailed with Essex's expedition to Cadiz in 1596.

ELEGIES

The Elegies are in some ways Donne's most characteristic poems. They reveal a nature at once passionate, restless, moody, violent, tender, idealistic and cynical. They are witty and profound; loose and informal in construction—they might be called, to use a term from music, 'Impromptus'.

49. ELEGIE IV: THE PERFUME

This Elegy describes Donne's secret courtship of a
young lady, it is not known who, with a suspicious bed-
ridden mother, and a suspicious, violent, coarse and
drunken father, who employs a gigantic and blas-
phemous porter to keep watch over her. Donne is
frankly interested in the wealth she will inherit at her
father's death. The atmosphere, marvellously re-
created in Donne's nervous, irregular couplets, is one of
close excitement and intrigue. The grim and savage
humour does not lessen the intensity of the feeling, for
those who can understand the many-sidedness of Donne's
nature. What gives Donne away is a "loud perfume";
and after describing the lovers' successful evasion of
both parents and porter, he ends with an embittered
denunciation of perfumes in general.

escapes: sins or faults.

Hydroptique: literally "afflicted with dropsy", but
Donne probably means "given to drink".

glazed: staring.

Cockatrice: fabulous serpent which killed by looking.

Thy beauties beautie . . . hope of his goods: her father
has threatened to cut her off from her chief attraction,
her inheritance.

ingled: were fondled.

But as wee in our Ile . . . just as those living among
cattle and dogs would suppose the precious unicorn
strange if it appeared, so your father was suspicious
of my perfume, having previously known only common
smells.

I taught my silkes . . . speechlesse were: compare *King
Lear*, III, iv, 97—"Let not the creaking of shoes nor the
rustling of silks betray thy poor heart to woman."

excrement: growth.

seely Amorous: simple lover.

51. ELEGIE V: HIS PICTURE

Written to his mistress before setting out on a military expedition, possibly that under Essex to Cadiz in 1596. Let his portrait, he says, remind her, after he returns broken and weather-beaten, of what he was like when she first loved him. But let her not disdain him for his coarse appearance, since their love should by then be strong enough to disregard external attractions.

'*Tis like me now ... than 'twas before:* if I am killed, my picture and I, being both shadows, will resemble each other even more than now.

52. ELEGIE IX: THE AUTUMNALL

This graceful tribute to the beauty of a mature woman is usually taken to be addressed to Lady Magdalen Herbert when a widow.

Anachorit: hermit.

Xerxes strange Lydian love: on his march to Greece, Xerxes honoured a plane-tree in Lydia by decorating it with gold ornaments and appointing a guardian.

To vexe their soules: it was believed that at the Resurrection the various parts of the body would come together; if some of the teeth were lost, the soul would be troubled.

lation: motion.

53. ELEGIE XII: HIS PARTING FROM HER

The subject of this poem, separation from a mistress (her identity is not known), always inspires Donne to his most intense and impassioned writing. No other poet can express so feelingly, in tone, language and even rhythm, the pangs of separation. This poem, like many others, is best appreciated when read aloud; like others of the *Elegies*, it is a sort of dramatic monologue. It is essential to remember that in addressing various objects

(Night, Love, etc.) Donne changes from one to another without warning.

Cinthia: the moon.

strange torments: the inner fires of love suggest to Donne the apparatus of torture (the Martyr's death at the stake, breaking on a wheel).

for forme: for fashion's sake.

thy husbands towring eyes: some editors read *lowring,* but Grierson explains *towring* as meaning "like a hawk about to swoop".

Shadow'd . . . most respects? Disguised our dearest hopes and desires under a mask of indifference.

under-boards: under the table.

Time shall not lose our passages: time itself will not be lacking in illustrations of our intercourse.

Though cold and darkness . . . and so we may: the cold and darkness of some parts of the earth are compensated for by warmth and light in other parts. So we can enjoy love's happiness even though parted for a time.

The Poles . . . ere I start: the earth's poles shall move before I become inconstant.

many words . . . perswade: to protest my constancy too much might throw suspicion on my sincerity.

56. ELEGIE XVI: ON HIS MISTRIS

It is probable that Donne is here addressing his wife, Anne More. He is about to cross the Continent for Italy, and it was evidently suggested that she might accompany him disguised as a page. Grierson notes that this was done by Elizabeth Southwell in 1605, when she accompanied Sir Robert Dudley. Donne begs her, in the name of all their past love, not to desire to accompany him; it would be madness to risk her life. The French would recognise her as a woman and assault her; the Italians would make love to her even though they thought her a boy; neither they nor the besotted Dutch would attack her if she remained in England. Of this passage Grierson writes: "The whole of these central lines reveal that strange bad taste, some radical want of delicacy which mars not only Donne's poems and lighter prose but even at times the sermons." Perhaps this is to judge a Renaissance writer by standards which had not yet come into existence.

Donne ends by urging her to stay in England and not tempt fate by imagining him in danger.

Boreas: the wind that brings storms at sea.

Orithea: wife of Boreas, the North wind.

and as soone Ecclips'd . . . Moone: just as we call the moon the moon, even in eclipse, so you would be known as a woman even in disguise.

Lot: the Hebrew patriarch whose life in Sodom, city of unnatural vice, is recounted in the book of Genesis.

England . . . Gallerie: England is the only fitting antechamber for you to live in before God calls you.

EPITHALAMIONS

59. ON THE LADY ELIZABETH AND COUNT PALATINE

Princess Elizabeth, daughter of James I and Anne of Denmark, was married to Frederick, Count Palatine, on St. Valentine's Day, February 14th, 1613, with great magnificence.

I   *chirping Choristers:* St. Valentine's Day is the day on which the birds choose their mates.

II.   *two Phœnixes:* the Phœnix was a fabulous bird of great rarity.

III.   *Thy starres:* the bride's hair and train, as well as those of her bridesmaids, were so ornamented with jewels that a contemporary compared her appearance to the Milky Way.

VIII.   *Nature againe restored is:* according to legend
there was only one Phœnix; their union would make the
Prince and Princess one and so restore to these "two
Phœnixes" their original uniqueness.

HOLY SONNETS

63. I.   A grave and despairing appeal to God to sustain
him as he feels death approaching.

63. II.   He belongs to God by right, yet he feels that
God has abandoned him and only the Devil seeks him.

64. III.   The remembrance of past pleasures comforts
the ordinary sinner at the approach of misfortune: in his
"idolatry" (i.e., his sinful youth) his sighs and tears
were wasted, because he was not, as now, truly repentant.
Now that he is sincerely converted to religion, he feels
the need for those sighs and tears he wasted before.

64. IV.   An agonised cry for the grace without which he
cannot begin to be truly repentant and so save his soul
from damnation.

65. V.   The subject is the same as that of the preceding.
He prays for Christian zeal to burn up his soul, as it had
formerly been burnt by the lusts of youth.

65. VI.   Convinced that he is about to die, he imagines
his body returning to the earth, his sins to hell, and his
soul to Heaven.

66. VII.   From a lofty and imaginative contemplation of
the Day of Judgement, when at the sound of angelic
trumpets the souls and bodies of all the dead shall be

reunited, Donne sinks to the humble contemplation of his own miserable lot. His sins exceed all other men's; let him be given grace to repent before it is too late.

66. VIII.   How will the saints and angels be able to distinguish my sincere repentance from the feigned grief of hypocrites? Only God can judge of my sincerity.

67. IX.   If plants, stones and animals are not damned for their wickedness, since they lack reason and intention, why should I be? Yet I must accept the will of God and pray for his mercy.

67. X.   Death is not the all-powerful tyrant it is sometimes called. It is itself the servant of "Fate, Chance, kings, and desperate men", and will in the end give way to eternal life.

68. XI.   An impassioned and self-reproachful assertion of the infinite love of God, who suffered in Christ's form the punishments due to man for his sins.

68. XII.   It is a wonder that nature should be subject to man, who is more sinful and corrupt; it is an even greater wonder that the creator himself should have died for men.
  seelily: foolishly.

69. XIII.   The beauty of Christ's face on the cross is a guarantee of his mercy and forgiveness. In introducing into such a poem as this the references to the "profane mistresses" of his "idolatry", is Donne guilty of the bad taste noted by Grierson (see note on *Elegie XVI*, p. 99)?

69. XIV.   In a series of brilliant paradoxes Donne begs God to take possession of his heart. None of his poems is more characteristic than this, with its nervous, jerky

rhythm, intensity of feeling, and violent, almost over-strained language.

70. XV.   The argument is briefly: God made man in his own image, to be a sharer in his glory; having lost man through man's transgressions, he was forced to buy him back again, as a robbed man has to buy back his own goods or lose them. This he did by giving his son, Christ, the likeness of man.

70. XVI.   This attempt to combine legal and theological arguments is obscure and involved. The conclusion is that, in order to be a partaker in God's kingdom, man must obey his laws; but since no man can do this wholly, God's love and mercy must make allowance for man's shortcomings.

71. XVII.   Here Donne refers to the death of his wife, Anne, in 1617. Since her death, he says, he has sought only the love of God, the source of his love for his wife. Although he is thirsty for God's love, God woos his soul on behalf of her who is in Heaven, and is jealous lest Donne's love should revert to the world, the flesh, and the devil.

71. XVIII.   Donne was ordained priest in the Church of England in 1615. All his life his loyalty had been divided between the Protestant Church of his country and the Roman Church of his parents. These doubts are reflected in this sonnet. The church is the Bride of Christ. Is it to be found, he asks, across the Channel in France and Italy or in Germany and England? He asks Christ to reveal his true bride, since he is happiest when all men court her.

   rob'd: robbed

72. XIX.   Donne frankly confesses that he is as incon-
stant in his devotion to God as he had been as a young
man in love. His wavering devotion is like a fever;
except that his best (i.e., most religious) moments are
those when he trembles most with the fear of God.

humorous: moody, changeable.

72. GOODFRIDAY, 1613. RIDING WESTWARD

In medieval cosmology the spheres were a set of
invisible spherical orbits in which moved the planets,
each with its attendant angel or "intelligence". The
primum mobile (first mover) was an outer sphere which
gave motion to all the others.

Donne calls his soul a sphere whose attendant angel
is devotion. The *primum mobile* is pleasure or business.
When on Good Friday his soul should be tending to-
wards the east, where Christ died, pleasure or business
causes him to ride westward, turning his back on the
dead Christ.

In the east he would see the dead Christ who, by the
forgiveness of man's sins, assured him eternal life—a
sight almost unbearable, since the death of Christ
involves the death of sinful man. Nature itself recoils
at the crucifixion, and the sight of the creator himself
thus suffering is intolerable. So also Donne finds the
thought of Christ's mother unbearable; yet these
things are fixed in his memory as he rides away, and he
turns his back on Christ only to be punished. When he
has been punished sufficiently, he will turn and face
Christ once more, and Christ will recognise him.

74. A HYMNE TO GOD THE FATHER

It is clear that in this poem Donne is punning on his
own name. In his time this was not inconsistent with
the most solemn thoughts. In his life of Donne, Izaak
Walton quotes this hymn, and adds: "I have the rather
mentioned this *Hymn*, for that he caus'd it to be set

to a most grave and solemn Tune, and to be often sung to the *Organ* by the *Choristers* of St. *Paul's* Church, in his own hearing; especially at the Evening Service, and at his return from his Customary Devotions in that place, did occasionally say to a friend, *The words of this* Hymn *have restored to me the same thoughts of joy that possest my Soul in my sickness when I composed it. And, O the power of Church-musick! that Harmony added to this Hymn has raised the Affections of my heart, and quickened my graces of zeal and gratitude;* and I observe, *that I always return from paying this publick duty of* Prayer and Praise *to God with an unexpressible tranquillity of mind,* and a willingness *to leave the world.*"

INDEX OF TITLES AND FIRST LINES